How to Open Your Own Shop or Gallery

How to Open Your Own Shop or Gallery

Leta W. Clark

St. Martin's Press
New York

44844

Also by Leta W. Clark

How to Make Money with Your Crafts
Women Women Women: Quips, Quotes
and Commentary

Library of Congress Cataloging in Publication Data

Clark, Leta W.
　　How to open your own shop or gallery.

　　Bibliography: p.
　　Includes index.
　　1. Small business—Handbooks, manuals, etc.
2. Self-employed—Handbooks, manuals, etc.　I. Title.
HF5356.C535　　　658.1'1　　　78-3981
ISBN 0-312-39607-4

Contents

44844

Preface

Writing this book was a delight—and sheer drudgery. For the past four years I've been teaching crafts marketing and have searched diligently for a text I could use that incorporated down-to-earth guidelines for opening a small store. I've read many volumes and have never ended up feeling I had enough of a grasp of the subject to open my own shop. The conclusion was obvious; I'd better write my own.

The research began. I interviewed, taped, corresponded, summarized and still felt a bit foggy. What finally brought it all together was a stint working in Gee, The Kids Need Clothes, a Greenwich Village children's boutique. Theory became actuality. Each day after the shop closed I would race to the typewriter, tear the manuscript apart and begin again.

Bit by bit the book got written. I found to my surprise that I had a natural bent—a talent, perhaps—for shopkeeping. I mentioned this delightful fact to my father, Stanley L. Wang, who replied, "Of course. It's heredity. You come from a long line of shopkeepers."

He described his mother, Caroline Swanby, a young girl in Comstock, Wisconsin, in the 1870s, running the family trading post when her father was off ferrying timber down the Mississippi. In addition to the local Norwegian settlement, the Indians were her big customers; in troubled times she slept with a rifle next to her bed ready to protect her younger sisters and brothers.

And he talked about his father, Louis Wang, proprietor of L. H. Wang's General Store, in Shell Lake, Wisconsin. One 1895 newspaper ad for the general store remains, reprinted by the *Washburn County Register* in their Bicentennial issue. The ad copy reads:

A Horrible Cut! Down They Go!
Men's Suits for $4.00
Boy's Suits for $1.75.
Everything You Want!
I Keep an All-Round Store
and
Carry a Full Stock of
EVERYTHING.

L. H. Wang

Pa hastened to remind me that in addition to owning the general store, Louis Wang was the sheriff and one of the founders of the Shell Lake town bank.

So much for talent. With lineage like this, how could I miss? I'm pleased with the book. It says what I wanted it to say, with a clarity the subject demands.

L. W. C.
JULY 1978

Acknowledgments

My sincere thanks to old and new friends for the help and encouragement they gave me; with special "above and beyond" citations to Doris Keefe Horovitz, Nicholas Tannone, Dick Ippoliti, Ugo Carlotti, Mark and Wanda Hanlon, Reva Calesky, Warren Hadler, and my children, Catherine, Mills and Caroline Clark.

1

Be Sure
It's What
You Want to Do

"I kept making things and making things and people would come see and want to buy, so I ended up opening a shop in self-defense. At least visiting hours would be restricted!"

"The two of us were talking about how there were no good children's stores nearby, and shopping uptown was such a drag. So we decided to open a small shop and carry all the things we'd buy for our own kids."

"I'd been in personnel for fifteen years and I just got fed up and quit. I had some money in the company credit union and the pension plan, so I decided to take it and open a shop. I've always been fascinated by rare teas and coffees, so I figured it's now or never—I've got the time, the money and the interest."

"I knew I'd have to get a job as soon as the divorce came

through, and I didn't think anyone would hire me. So I decided to open a small boutique. After all, I'd spent enough years shopping in them so I knew what made them good or bad."

"I'd worked in shops on and off since I was a kid. It was always just a way to pick up extra money until one day—and I don't know why—I took a close look at what was going on. The shop I was in was very successful, always crowded, doing great business. At the end of each day there was a lot of money in the register, yet I was still getting my $3.50 an hour like the rest of the help. That did it. From then on I started planning for my own shop where I would get a larger slice of the pie."

Do any of these tales sound familiar? They're some of the countless reasons people have for opening a shop. The motivations come from many sources, but they all have in common a sense of personal urgency—Do it and Do It Now! The person generally feels that the moment for action has arrived.

One of the actions you've already taken is to begin reading this book. Let your next action be to draw up a worksheet of your current resources, expectations and circumstances. In other words, before you do much else, make sure opening a shop is really what you want to do.

Small business is a tricky game. The owner must double as real estate operator, buyer, window decorator, bookkeeper, salesclerk, cleaning person, advertising agency and more. Dreary statistics are readily available documenting the high mortality rate of fledgling retailers. According to the United States Small Business Administration, the current nationwide failure rate of women's boutiques is 75 percent. Dun & Bradstreet, in their study "Business Failure Record Through 1973," found that 58 percent of all business failures in the United States in 1971 were in the retail trade.

The Dun & Bradstreet survey goes on to pinpoint 92.2 percent of these failures as being brought about by inexperience and incompetence, areas that include inadequate sales, competitive weakness, heavy operating expenses, receivables difficulties, inventory difficulties, excessive fixed assets and poor location.

It gives one pause. On the other hand, some people go into business and succeed. They do it and do it well. What makes the difference?

A good starting place is to examine the availability of free time in your life. Do you really have the time to devote to a shop? Unbelievably long hours put into the business are a characteristic of retailing. Family life, social life and all other obligations are bound to suffer during the first few years a new shop is open. Consider how many hours in your week are actually available to put into your business. What other demands are made on your time and what changes would have to be made in your life? In other people's lives?

Mobility is closely related to time. If you are homebound with small children or the elderly, your access to markets and suppliers is curtailed. Is private transportation or public transportation readily available? Merchandise will have to be picked up and packages mailed off, banking must be done. Will any of these be a problem in your current circumstances?

Look carefully at your finances. Each year the cost of setting up a small shop has risen, and there's no indication that this trend will reverse itself. You will need money and lots of it—money that you can afford to lose. Business is as much a gamble as a horse race. It's great to win, but how much can you afford to lose?

How about experience? Have you ever worked in a shop for any length of time? Your planning will be helped if you have done something similar.

If you have no in-store experience try to arrange some, even as an unpaid volunteer. It will help sort out your feelings about spending hour after hour in a shop, coping with boredom, customers, crowds, shoplifters, pets and deliveries. Obviously no activity as varied as retailing will be 100 percent delightful, but after several weeks "on the floor" you'll know pretty well whether or not it's your cup of tea.

The last, and perhaps most important, area to explore is your own inner qualifications for the job. Running any small business takes a lot of tenacity, decisiveness, assertiveness. Without such qualities inherent in the management, a shop will need constant financial and emotional bolstering, and seldom becomes a money-making proposition.

Fill in the following questionnaire to formulate a picture of your own adaptability to becoming a small-business entrepreneur. There are no right or wrong answers. The real question is how you respond to the types of pressure common to small-business management.

There are no scoring directions. Your answers will serve as an inventory of your likes and dislikes, showing how comfortable you can expect to be when running a small business.

If your answers indicate that you are easily manipulated by others, or tend to withdraw when faced with unpleasantness, you may want to restructure some of your old habits and behavior patterns. In the past few years the study of assertiveness and assertiveness training have become a part of the behavioral sciences. Listed in the Appendix of this book are a number of excellent resources, including several books that are used as texts for assertiveness training. Within the Women's Movement there are assertiveness-training workshops offered in many parts of the country. Check your local National Organization for Women (NOW) office for details.

QUESTIONNAIRE

1. List the three leisure-time activities you most enjoy.
   _____

2. During your last two years of schooling what extracurricular activities did you participate in? _____
   _____

3. Which individual sports are you currently active in?
   _____

4. Which team sports? _____
   _____

5. List community activities in which you have taken part in the past five years. _____
   _____

6. List leisure-time activities you participate in that you least enjoy. _____
   _____

7. List three parts of your day-to-day living that you would like to avoid. _____
   _____

8. How would you rate your health?
   Excellent _____ Fair _____
   Good _____ Poor _____

9. How often did you consult a physician during the past two years? _____
   _____

10. How many hours each week could you devote to your shop? _____

11. What other demands are made on your time?_____

_____

12. How would you estimate your personal mobility?

_____

13. How much money do you have to invest?
    Under $1000 _____
    $1000 to $5000 _____
    $5000 to $10,000 _____

14. Do you keep your checkbook balanced and in good order? _____

15. List your last two paying jobs. _____

_____

16. What did you like most and what did you like least about these jobs? _____

_____

17. What business skills do you have?_____

_____

18. List two events (business, community or social) that you organized or ran. _____

_____

_____

19. How would you rate yourself as an administrator?
    Good _____
    Fair _____
    Poor _____

20. Do you make decisions easily? _____

21. Do you speak out when you consider someone is unfair? _____

_____

22. Are you able to refuse unreasonable requests made by friends? _____

23. Do you find it difficult to maintain eye contact when you talk to others? _____

24. Can you give constructive criticism easily? _____

25. Do you tend to avoid people or situations you feel will

be difficult to handle or embarrassing? _____

26. Can you hold your temper? _____
27. Do you become defensive when blamed for mistakes?
28. Are you able to identify and resist high-pressure tactics? _____
    _____
29. Can you supervise others and delegate authority? _____
30. How would you rate your performance under pressure?

    Good _____
    Fair _____
    Poor _____

31. How much money do you need to make per year (clear profit) to feel that your business is worth all the trouble? _____
32. What is your business goal in five years? _____
    _____

    _____

Read over your answers and look for conclusions you can draw about your behavior patterns. Perhaps you will conclude that, given free choice, you

> gravitate toward solo pursuits rather than team activities
> are more sedentary than exuberantly active
> rarely slip into the role of organizer or leader
> tend to move away from confrontation rather than to instigate it

Or perhaps you will find the reverse, that you

> have always ended up leading the team
> hate to work solo
> speak out at every turn
> perform best under pressure

The value of these conclusions comes when you compare them with what retailers say about running their own shops. Over 300 retailers were surveyed in depth for this book, and when interviews were compared, I found that certain characteristics cropped up in almost every dialogue. A composite picture of the ideal store owner would include the following:

Flexibility	The ability to move smoothly through diverse happenings; deal with the unexpected.
Outgoingness	You are meeting people constantly; it really helps if you genuinely like them.
Self-Confidence	Liking yourself is also important—believing in yourself, standing up for what you believe.
Decisiveness	Think twice about retailing if you agonize over every decision; a constant changing of direction is taboo.
Administrative Ability	The ability to organize time and space: to keep final control over everything but still be able to utilize the talents and strengths of others.
Physical Strength	Good health and lots of energy are imperative.
Unlimited Time	There are no nine-to-five days and few weekends and holidays, at least during the first five years. Total immersion is the norm, with all other responsibilities taking a back seat.

Resistance to boredom	There are long stretches of isolation and boredom as you sit alone in the shop day after day—then meet frenzied activity during peak buying hours. This kind of "home alone" feeling can be demoralizing.
Money	Access to it and respect for it; the ability to see money as just another commodity that you buy, sell, rent and acquire.

Review your questionnaire answers with the above nine points as a comparison. Remember, there are no right or wrong answers. Every human being is unique, and individuality is one of the nicest things about being a person. Use the survey to help you focus and prepare for what is ahead.

2

Research

Once you've made the decision to open a shop, it's tempting to rush right out and start doing things. Well, don't. Your chances of success increase greatly if you take the time to do some market research.

Gauging your competition takes top priority. Even though you might feel your shop will be unlike any other known to Western man, accept the fact that you will have competition. You need to know as much about those competitors as you can. Your observations will be of help to you in planning specifics and in making decisions about your own operation. Find out what they're doing so you can do it better.

Locate competition any way you can. Walks through your area, drives into neighboring towns, careful looks through shopping centers, local newspapers, the phone book, the local Chamber of Commerce, the visitor's bureau—all can add to your knowledge of your bailiwick.

Large retailers often break down their competitors into primary (local) or secondary (nonlocal but within 10 miles) and tertiary (10 to 25 miles). Twenty-five miles seems to be the outer limits of true competition.

Once you have chosen a location, plan a series of visits to the competition. You may or may not choose to identify yourself as a potential shop owner; that's up to you. Much of what you need to know won't involve conversation. You're going out to observe and then compare.

What you want to see is the inner structure of the competitor's business. Bring a small notebook, prepared before setting out, so all you need to do on location is to fill in the blanks. Put a competitor's name and address on each page, and then list the following:

> Outside appearance
> Identification (signs, banners)
> Approximate size
> Display windows
> Inner appearance
> Size of selling area
> Lighting
> Inner displays
> Whether prices are displayed
> Price range in shop
> Merchandise range
> Time visited
> Traffic
> Comments

The first four headings deal with the exterior, providing data on what impression the shop gives as you approach it. Is it easy to understand what kind of shop it is? Is it clean and inviting? Are the hours clearly stated?

The next four categories tell you about the atmosphere inside: the general feeling you get when you walk in. Small/crowded or small/delightfully cozy? Dark/dreary or bright/sparkly? Is the merchandise displayed attractively and can you reach it easily? Make note of what your eye is drawn to first as you enter, and decide why you focused there first. What merchandise is up front and what is kept in the back? Are there chairs available?

The next three items are crucial. Can you readily see the many different kinds of merchandise sold or do you have to ask for help? Do you have to ask prices? Is there a markdown rack or table? How easy is it for a customer to actually buy something in this shop?

The next two listings are your own traffic study, important because you might be serving the same geographic area. Visit each competitor's shop several days at different hours to see which are the busy selling hours and which are the slack times. Note street traffic. Do lots of people walk by the shop? Do many stop at the display windows? Do many go in? Do they come out with purchases?

Take into consideration the nature of the street traffic. If everybody's hurrying to work, they have no time to stop and buy. However, shops located near bus stops always benefit from street traffic.

Add your personal comments. Were you made to feel welcome, or did you feel you were intruding? Was there anything especially pleasant? Or especially unpleasant?

Then, look over all the filled-in notebook pages and start evaluating your data. From the do's and dont's of your competitors you'll be able to clarify some of your thinking. Let the things that work well do the same for you, and steer clear of the negatives. That can be your first profit—from the mistakes of others.

For one thing, you can try to figure out who the typical customer is that each of these places wants to attract. Who are they really in business to serve? Successful retailers, both large and small, know they will make more sales by aiming for one segment of the population and really catering to the needs and tastes of that group than if they try to be everything to everybody.

Major department stores have made almost a science out of defining their ideal customer so they can then design everything from displays to shopping bags and bill enclosures to appeal to her. The imaginary customer profile includes age bracket, sex, income level, marital status, family structure, social life, reading habits and living conditions.

For example, for years one leading New York City department store catered to the elegant, affluent, "settled-down" lady. Not surprisingly, the logo, or symbol, of that store—which decorated everything from shopping bags to the ladies' room decor—was a tasteful nosegay of violets, lavender ribbons streaming.

See if you can envision the ideal customer your competitors are trying to attract. Will their ideal customer also be yours? What can you do to sharpen the focus of the ideal customer so she'll head for your shop like a homing pigeon?

Spend a little time drawing up your own customer profile. Define age and income, family situation and some specific ways you can create a shop that will be especially attractive to this customer. For example, if you plan to cater to young marrieds, you might find it advantageous to include a children's play area in your floor plan. You know what your competitors are doing; now make some plans to do it better.

Your next bit of research might be to visit your Chamber of Commerce to pick up any data they have on population, traffic flow, local store hours, buying patterns, holidays and special events. You might want to use this visit to introduce yourself to the Chamber of Commerce as a potential member. Get data on meeting schedules and the advantages of membership. Often this is an ideal way to break the ice with the local business community.

Plan research time at your local library for two areas:

business and retailing resource material and current consumer and trade periodicals that show styles and trends in your field.

The word *trade* includes everyone connected with the creating, producing, selling or promoting of consumer goods. As a retailer you will be part of the trade. The counterpart of the trade person is the consumer, the person who buys an item for his or her own personal use, not to resell it to somebody else. The consumer is the end of the line for all trade activities, and all trade activities are in some way related to attracting and servicing the consumer.

Every type of business or trade has its own reading material, from the legendary *Women's Wear Daily* down to small, specialized publications such as the *Handcrafter's Newsletter—the How-to, Where-to, What's-new Monthly Crafts Newsletter*. If you are not familiar with the trade publications in your field, check the library's copy of *Reader's Guide to Periodical Literature* and write to publishers for sample copies of whatever sounds pertinent.

It is important to keep yourself informed of trends, marketing news, new creative influences or designers and raw materials. Also, by reading your trade papers regularly you will build up an understanding and a vocabulary of your field that can't be acquired any other way.

Excellent trade reading material also comes from the United States government through the smallest of the federal agencies—the Small Business Administration. The S.B.A. was set up by Congress in 1953 to "support and promote small business and to be totally responsive to the needs of the small business community." Facilities of the S.B.A. are located throughout the country: 82 regional offices plus many branches bring the wealth of S.B.A. resources within the reach of almost every citizen. (See Appendix for addresses of S.B.A. offices.)

The S.B.A. publications are written by experts in every field and cover many diverse topics. Some typical pamphlets: *The ABC's of Borrowing, Steps in Meeting Your Tax Obligations, Marketing Checklist for Small Retailers, Financial Record Keeping for Small Stores* and *Handbook of Small Business Finance*.

Contact your local S.B.A. office and ask them to send you the free publications listings of management aids and for-sale booklets. Some of these booklets are free, others are sold at minimal cost.

Consumer publications are the magazines you and everybody else reads for fun. Except that now you're going to start reading them for fun and profit, checking out what the buying public is being told is desirable, chic, stylish, comfortable, convenient and important. The printed word has an eerie authority about it. Powerful magazines feature a trend, a color or a product, and consumers listen. And they buy—at your shop or somebody else's.

Go back to your ideal customer profile and start looking through the magazines you feel he or she is reading. Skip the advertisements that fill the front and the back of every magazine, and concentrate on the editorial pages in the center of the book. It's there that the "run right out and buy" and "you really need to get this" message comes through. Your customers' buying habits are influenced by what they read, so monitor these messages on a regular basis and take advantage of the "pre-sell."

Finding the physical shop that is perfect for you, or at least acceptable to you, requires research. Location is all-important. The considerations here are two: how much you feel you can afford and how much you will have to spend to be in the right place. A dynamite shop in a ghastly location makes no more sense than a tacky, bare-boned storefront in the fashionable part of town.

Many beginning retailers predicate their projected rent figure on what they think they could afford to carry if their shop made no money at all for a while. "Better be pessimistic than sorry" is their theory, and it works—but only when the amount of money they pay for rent allows them to locate in the area where they can do the best business. A few calls to real estate agents will bring information about typical rents in the "right" part of town.

Finding a spot close to the center of the business district guarantees you high traffic. And as a general rule, shops that appeal to the same type of customer increase each other's sales. Statistics on future building plans for an area will be helpful; an apartment complex on the drawing board can double or triple your potential customers within a few years.

Accessibility is another vital factor. No matter where you locate, your business volume will be in direct proportion to how convenient it is for your customers to shop there. Parking facilities are often the *bête noir* of city retailers. Locating near public transportation routes is a plus.

The amount of renovation needed to turn the space into what you envision as your kind of shop needs consideration. Sometimes landlords are willing to undertake part of the renovation if it is in line with permanent improvements.

When a building owner advertises he "will divide to suit," he is giving notice that *all* structural changes will be undertaken by him, leaving the tenants a new, freshly painted interior into which to move their fixtures and merchandise. The "divide to suit" statement normally covers the interior of the space only; refurbishing the exterior and front entrance is up to the tenants.

Over the past ten years there has been an increase in what city planners refer to as secondary business districts.

Many of these house small, distinctive shops developed in relation to historic-restoration areas, urban redevelopment projects or cultural and educational centers. Secondary business districts, in addition to having a cluster of unusual stores and restaurants, generally have lower rents.

When considering these areas one thing to check on is the customer traffic flow during whatever you have in mind as your regular work hours. Often the main crush of potential customers depends on special events scheduled within the area, or weekend browsers out to stroll in pleasant weather. Talk to the shop owners already operating there. Also find out the number and types of businesses that tried and failed. High-volume stores need consistently high traffic.

Another type of secondary business district is the shopping mall, be it quaint and historic or new and chrome-plated. These one-stop shopping centers work on the theory that a few major stores generate traffic, and "necessity" shops, such as drug stores, pick up local convenience business. Added to these are little specialty shops to add diversity and flavor. All businesses feed off the major stores' clientele, so the customer profile of the giants should be in line with your own.

Shopping-mall space normally is rented a bit differently from that in other locations. The amount is figured on a percentage of the gross sales over and above a dollars-per-square-foot base rent. For example, a small, 30- to 45-store shopping center might charge 6 or 7 percent of each shop's gross sales over and above a $5-per-square-foot base rental. Or a larger mall might require up to 9 percent of gross sales on top of a base rent of $8 or $9 per square foot of space.

It is not unusual to find additional contributory charges required by a shopping mall. Most common is a monthly fee for cleaning and maintenance of the area plus an advertising guarantee that each shop will run a certain amount of advertising, or a special-event contribution that covers promotion and decorations for holidays and special sales.

Shopping malls might seem attractive and worry-free, but they are seldom the ideal spot for the novice retailer. They are built to sustain high volume and they offer more than most beginners can handle, at higher prices than most beginners can afford.

Once you have narrowed down your choices to a few locations, do some research on what the lease arrangements might be. Leases are as good or as bad as you make them, so be prepared to dicker. There is no rigid formula, but be sure to discuss the following:

Alterations	Who pays; whose workers must be used?
Length of lease	Make it for a few years with an option for renewal for the next few. The option clause should state the rent, explaining built-in increases.
Cancellation clause	The landlord might ask for this so that he would have the right to get you out before your lease has run out. If you are faced with a cancellation clause, insist that it spells out protection for you, such as the amount of advance notice (in writing) you must be given, under what circumstances your lease could be cancelled, and how you would be reimbursed for renovations you've paid for. The reimburse-

ment is usually worked out on a sliding scale dating from when the work was done.

Sublease If you want out, how do you go about it? Do you find a new tenant at your own expense but subject to the landlord's approval? Who covers the rent if no subtenant can be found and for how long? What happens if the new tenant can only pay less than your lease calls for? Will you be expected to make up the difference, and for how long?

Protection In some parts of the country leases contain a description of the type of shop the tenant is going to have, and the landlord agrees to protect the tenant by not renting next-door space to an identical shop or even to a shop that would carry similar lines of merchandise.

Heat and air conditioning Who pays and what times and dates does the service begin and end? This is especially important if you plan to be open some evenings and weekends.

Repairs Who pays for what and whose workers do the job?

Insurance Who covers what and at what amounts?

Leases are tricky. It's a good idea to ask your lawyer, if

you have one, to go over any lease you are considering and check it out for pitfalls. However, if you're dealing for yourself remember: *always* ask for extra clauses that make the lease work better for you. Clauses are like diamonds—you might never use them but they're nice to have around.

3

Money—
How Much
Is Enough?

There are many ways of estimating how much your initial investment or initial capitalization should be. One thing is clear: there is never too much money, and nobody ever started without any money even if they produced their own inventory.

Estimates, by definition, are near guesses rather than hard facts. They can and should be tailored by you to fit your particular circumstances and special talents. The "necessities" for one shop may well be the nonessentials for another, so it is difficult to select one sure-fire formula.

This chapter will give you a jumping-off point from which to proceed, as you eliminate material you feel is not for you and add data that is more pertinent.

Expenses in retailing divide themselves into two categories: pre-opening expenses, which include everything it takes to get the door open on Day One, and monthly operating expenses, or everything you need to keep the shop operating.

The pre-opening expenses include the following:

> rent advance and security
> renovation of space
> fixtures and lighting
> exterior sign or banner
> advertising
> publicity
> freight and express charges
> telephone deposit
> utilities deposit
> supplies—e.g., paper bags, boxes, sales slips
> insurance
> legal and accounting fees
> inventory
> pre-opening sanitation and trash pick-up
> salaries, if any
> locks, security gates, alarm system
> miscellaneous

Monthly operating expenses include the following:

> rent
> heat/electricity
> advertising/promotion
> display materials
> supplies
> accountant
> telephone
> insurance
> window washer
> sanitation pick-up
> salaries
> repayment of loans or notes
> taxes
> miscellaneous

44844

Begin your financial planning by getting estimates of the flat fees, such as telephone and utilities deposits, costs of insurance, supplies when purchased in quantity, different-sized ads in local papers (more on advertising in Chapter 9.)

Gather as much free information as you can. Add your own educated guesses, backed up by builders' and contractors' estimates, on the space renovation, fixtures, lighting and exterior sign or banner.

Once you get an idea of costs, you need to start estimating how much business you are going to need to do in order to support all these expenses. In other words, how large a shop with how much inventory is necessary for you to make enough sales to cover expenses *and* make a profit? The reasoning at this point seems almost circular—it's the old chicken-or-egg story.

A key to the solution, which leads directly into inventory planning, is your *estimated average sale*. Once you establish your price range, you can figure out how many sales per week you need in order to ring up enough cash to make the shop function and flourish.

Begin inventory planning by making up preliminary lists of specific amounts of specific items you want to sell in your shop. "You can't do business from an empty wagon" is the old but true adage. A successful shop owner offers the customer the merchandise she wants to buy at the price she wants to pay and at the moment she wants to buy.

No matter what kind of shop you have, inventory is easier if handled in subdivisions. There is no one perfect method, but a commonly used guide is:

High-value items	Generally under 20 percent of the total quantity of stock, but

	representing up to 60 percent of the total dollar investment.
Medium-value items	The core of your inventory, accounting for 50 percent of the quantity of stock but only about 25 percent of the total dollar investment.
Low-value items	Approximately 30 percent of the quantity of your inventory but representing only about 15 percent of your inventory investment.

Within these subdivisions are the categories of merchandise you wish to deal with. For example, *Women's Wear Daily* recommends a merchandise category breakdown for a women's apparel shop as follows:

50 percent items that are the basic stock in the shop, containing the main fashion "look" and making the major fashion statement to the customers.

25 percent seasonal goods, showing the latest fashion trends which may or may not appeal to the bulk of the customers but which, when displayed, make the shop look up-to-date and fashion-wise.

15 percent accessories, generally within the taste boundaries of the basic stock.

10 percent fad, promotional items, gimmicky apparel or accessories, perhaps to be sold at lower prices or as "special purchases."

Within each of these categories there should be a high-value, a medium-value and a low-value group.

Sizing brings up yet another complication to inventory planning: how much of which sizes do you need in order to bring the customer what she wants when she wants it? A rule of thumb often given by retailers is to stock "one-two-two-one," which translates into deciding which *two* sizes will be most desired by your customers, and stocking them double the amount that you stock the two sizes on either side. For example:

Size 8	one item
Size 10	two items
Size 12	two items
Size 14	one item

This explains why very big and very little people go batty trying to find good selections and often travel miles to specialty stores that cater only to their sizes.

Consult with your wholesalers and suppliers about size mixes. They have the most accurate, up-to-date information on what will go best together and what is most commonly stocked in shops aimed at various kinds of customers. Here, again, your customer profile is important.

A final point with inventory planning is the amount of turnover you can realistically expect. This will help determine how much money you must put into stock initially. Turnover means the number of times in one year any one item is purchased by a customer and then replaced in stock by you, the retailer.

The *Barometer of Small Business* quotes 1973 inventory turnover in the retail trade as:

Gift and novelty shops	2.3 times per year
Children's and infants' apparel	4.26 times per year
Women's specialty (apparel)	2.38 times per year
Jewelry stores	1.7 times per year

The obvious stock turnover times for shops selling apparel are fall/winter and spring/summer, times when major changes in clothing weights are needed. Too few stock turnovers result in a shop filled with dated merchandise that customers have already seen on previous visits.

An exception is the tourist-oriented shop, whose customers pass by only once, so the stock always looks fresh, and repeat business is unlikely.

It pays to be extremely realistic when estimating your inventory turnover. Unsold inventory represents cash tied up and unusable, whether for purchases of new items or other uses. It's easy to push up inventory turnover by carrying very little merchandise so everything that gets sold must be reordered and replaced. However, bare shelves and empty racks make a shop look marginal, scare customers away and build a reputation for never having much of a selection. Best plan your opening inventory in modest depth to give customers some choice.

The size of the shop must be considered in relation not only to depth of inventory but to overall sales potential. Obviously a tiny place has limited potential for numbers of sales per day. People who stand in line willingly to get into the local ice cream store seldom wait in line to get into a boutique. When you are considering floor space, larger is better within any one rent level, and the threat of outgrowing the location is lessened.

Most shops, however, look more attractive with lots of inventory, giving the customer the impression that the place is just brimming with goodies. Movable display and counter units can help concentrate a thin inventory toward the front of a large space and create a workroom or studio or merely extra storage in the rear.

For your initial financial estimating, try to arrive at a dollar figure that represents what you hope will be your average sale, based on your inventory lists. The medium-value core of stock is what you're offering most, so your figure will fall somewhere in there.

Wholesale prices are generally doubled to get the retail figure—e.g., an item you buy from a wholesale supplier for $5 would be marked up and sold in your shop for $10. In retailing jargon this doubling is referred to as "keyston-ing" and is the accepted way to arrive at a retail price for goods such as apparel, home fashions and accessories. Other fields have other markup ratios. You may find through experience that you can charge more than the usual markup on certain merchandise, but in your ad-vance planning stick to the average markup to simplify matters.

If you are making most of your own inventory, use any of the standard costing formulas to determine the best wholesale price—the price at which you would be willing to sell an item to another shopkeeper. (For more costing information see Chapter 7.)

To get all this information into usable shape, you now have to tally up some of the lists you've made and trans-late the summaries into a working plan. You first need to know a rough total of your pre-opening expenses, and then a total of your projected monthly operating expenses. Then, based on your average sales figure, some idea of in-ventory needed can be developed.

The summarizing can best be illustrated by setting up an example. Say you wanted to open a small children's-apparel boutique, and you have located a handsome space that measures about 240 square feet. Your tally sheets might look like these:

Pre-Opening Expenses (Excluding Inventory)

Rent advance (2 months)	$700.00
Rent security (1 month)	350.00
Renovations	1,000.00
Phone deposit	100.00
Utilities deposit	100.00
Supplies	500.00
Advertising/promotion	800.00
Legal & accounting (incorporating)	600.00
Locks and security gates	300.00
Sanitation	50.00
Insurance	200.00
SUBTOTAL	$4,700.00
MISCELLANEOUS, 6% OF TOTAL	282.00
TOTAL	$4,982.00
ROUNDED-OFF WORKING TOTAL	$5,000.00

The next group of figures to total are your estimates of what it will cost you to keep the shop open. This is figured on a monthly basis, and for the children's shop they would look something like the following:

Monthly Operating Expenses

Rent	$350.00
Advertising/promotion	25.00
Display	25.00
Supplies	75.00
Accountant	50.00
Telephone	35.00
Electricity	30.00
Sanitation/trash pick-up	10.00
Window washer	7.50

Insurance, payable quarterly	20.00
Salaries	760.00
Corporate taxes	10.00
City rent and occupancy tax	17.00
Miscellaneous	20.00
TOTAL	$1,434.50

ROUNDED-OFF WORKING TOTAL $1,500.00

Using the keystoning markup—i.e., doubling the wholesale cost of inventory—the children's shop would have to make $3,000 worth of retail sales in order to cover the operating expenses of $1,500. This is *not* allowing for any profit—the $3,000 worth of sales will merely keep the shop open and not running at a loss.

Based on the type of merchandise to be featured in the children's boutique, the average sale is estimated to be around $10. Therefore, 300 sales must be made each month in order to clear the $3,000 needed to cover expenses. This breaks down further into needing 75 sales per week at $10 per average sale. (Question here: Does the shop location look as if it has the buying traffic for 75 sales per week at about $10 per sale?)

The inventory planned for this children's shop features several categories of children's wear, each to be stocked in a depth in keeping with what the competition is offering. To make 300 sales each month, the shop owners decided that the customers should be offered a selection of five items to choose from. This was arrived at by observing the competition, reviewing their own inventory planning lists, checking with suppliers and attempting to figure out what stock they would have to show customers requesting specific categories, such as gifts for newborns, or sweatshirts.

The shop owners then multiplied the 300 monthly sales

figure by 5, coming up with 1,500 items they should have in the original stock. If their average retail sales figure is $10, their cost per sale comes to $5—what they would have to pay the wholesale supplier for the goods. Thus they could get a total inventory estimate:

1,500 different items needed to give each customer a choice of 5 pieces, multiplied by a cost of $5 per item:

$$1,500 \times \$5 = \$7,500 \text{ inventory}$$

The next step is to total up the three estimates:

Pre-opening Expenses	$5,000.00
Inventory	7,500.00
Monthly operating expenses	1,500.00
TOTAL	$14,000.00

New businesses can never rely on "making it" in one month's time. In order to ensure enough time for the shop to settle into a business routine, for customers to find the shop and become regular purchasers and for all the other breaking-in problems to be dealt with, retailers are strongly advised to bank enough capital to carry the shop for six months to a year at the break-even point.

Six months' coverage for operating expenses based on $1,500 per month changes the totals:

Six months' monthly expenses	$9,000.00
Original inventory	7,500.00
Pre-opening expenses	5,000.00
CAPITALIZATION NEEDED TO OPEN CHILDREN'S SHOP	$21,500.00

4

Ways to
Raise Money

Almost everybody has to raise money to open a shop. Basically there are two ways to do it:

Debt financing

You borrow cash. You pay back the amount plus an additional fee for interest. The money lender furnished only the cash, and you retain control of your business.

Equity financing

You sell shares in your business, giving other people a portion of control and/or potential profits. This can be done with shares of stock, or shares of partnership or limited partnership.

Debt financing can be a pretty casual thing. Every time you lend a friend taxi money you are, in effect, participating in debt financing, minus the fee for interest. One's family and friends are often the first approached for open-a-shop loans and usually the first to come through.

If you begin your borrowing on the home front, you can make life simpler if you draw up a one-page letter to use as a note setting out the terms of the loan. True, one's mother might not feel the need for "on-paper" terms, but the issuing of a written arrangement puts the transaction into a businesslike framework and may well be helpful as future proof of loans borrowed and repaid.

Make two copies, one for each of you, of a brief statement outlining the agreement. For example:

Date _____

To Whom It May Concern:

On the _____ day of (month) _____ ,
197_____ , I, _____ (your name) _____ ,
borrowed the total sum of $_____ (amount) _____
from _____ (name) _____ .

The loan is for_____ (number _____ years, due
on the_____ day of_____ (month) ____ , 197_____ ,
and can be renewed or repaid at that time.

(your name)
_____
(name)

If you both decide to have the loan paid off in small amounts over a period of time, use a final sentence such as:

The loan is for_____ (number) _____ years and
must be repaid at the rate of $_____ (amount) ____ every
_____ (month/quarter/year) ____ beginning on the_____
day of____ (month) _____ , 197_____ .

Allow yourself plenty of leeway in the payment arrangements with family and friends. If you borrow money six months in advance of your opening date, there is no way you can expect to begin paying back at least until income starts flowing in. The Small Business Administration estimates that in most retail businesses profit doesn't begin to accrue until the second year. Whenever possible give yourself extra time before you have to begin repayment of loans.

Many small businesses are opened on a combination of owner capital (the total amount you can come up with through private means) and bank-borrowed capital. The money you can borrow from a bank will be less than the money you can put up yourself and will come either as a personal loan or as a business loan.

Personal loans are the most likely for a new business person. These are the same loans you would take out if you wanted to buy a new car, take a vacation or have the kids' teeth straightened. The least expensive personal loan and the easiest one to get is the passbook loan, where you borrow against money you have in your savings account, using the savings as collateral. Discuss the types of personal loans available to you with officers at several local banks. Be sure to shop around.

Business loans, although much more difficult to get, are not out of the question for a new business person—provided you have over 50 percent of your own capital, a sizable amount of pertinent business experience, acceptable collateral to put up and somebody with a steady salary to cosign the loan. That salaried somebody does seem to be crucial and is often handled by having the salaried person become a silent partner. Working husbands or wives are ideal candidates.

There are a number of standard questions that need answering when you apply for a business loan. Some banks have worked out a "borrower's packet," with the forms and information pre-assembled to minimize the task. However you view it, business loan applications are extremely detailed and require a gigantic amount of paper work. You want to present as positive and convincing a proposal as you can put together.

Loan applications include:

Opening statement—what it is that you have in mind
Rationale—why you want to do it
Resumés—as though you were applying for a job
Personal statements—your own assets, liabilities, bank and insurance references, sources of income
Projected gross sales for the first year your shop is open,— showing estimated turnover figures for each category of merchandise you plan to sell
Projected earnings statements for several years
Monthly projected sales analysis for one year.

Then, if the loan officers are interested but dubious, you may be asked to prepare a second application based on a reduced amount of money and/or a reduced projected operation.

An example of a successful loan application is that of Joan and Bob Keefe of Ipswich, Massachusetts. They decided to open a book-and-record shop in Ipswich, about thirty miles north of Boston. The shop would also carry plants and reproductions of Shaker furniture, long a personal interest of the Keefes. The only competition at that time was one long-established bookshop that had de-emphasized books and was selling mostly gifts and knickknacks.

Joan quit her job with the Boston office of the Department of Health, Education and Welfare to spend time finding a good location and doing the preliminary work for their shop. Bob continued in his position as chairman of the English Department at the Ipswich High School. This gave them one salaried person in the partnership that was applying for the business loan. Their major asset was their home, which was still under a mortgage.

The Keefes found a suitable shop, got estimates on everything they could think of, tracked down suppliers interested in doing business with them and then spent weeks putting together the loan application asking for $16,000.

After much dickering and one major downward revision, the loan was granted—not for the hoped-for amount, but for $12,000 plus an additional $4,000 to cover the interest payments. That meant in reality they borrowed and were in debt for $16,000 but only had the use of $12,000. They were able to get extended credit from their suppliers to make up the difference, so the original plan of operation still worked despite the change in the bank loan.

Their opening statement read:

Shaker Tree

(Books, Records, Plants and Shaker Furniture)
Capital needs:

Renovations and fixtures	$6,000.00
Opening and inventory	10,000.00
Owner investment:	$5,000.00

Following the opening statement the Keffes offered their reasons why their shop would be a fine investment:

Shaker Tree

Rationale:

- No complete book, record or plant store in the community
- No similar store in surrounding communities (Topsfield, Essex, Hamilton, Wenham)

- Nearest serious competition is in Danvers, Peabody or Newburyport
- Distributors contacted will give terms allowing us to be competitive with larger stores like Lechmere and Paperback Booksmith
- Convenience for local patrons
- Money kept in own community
- Best location in town for maximum exposure to walking traffic (Market Street)
- Backgrounds of proprietors
- Awareness of current reading interests
- Awareness of current listening interests
- Ability of proprietors to deal with public
- Knowledge of plants (care, value, display)
- Knowledge of Shaker history and philosophy
- Familiarity with community residents for three years, one partner employee in school system for ten years
- Outstanding credit rating

The next part of the application packet was their resumés, filling the loan officers in on each of their backgrounds:

RESUMÉ

Joan Ead Keefe
Greens Point Road
Ipswich, Mass. 01938

Born and raised in Concord, Massachusetts

Educated in the Concord Public Schools and the College of Liberal Arts, Boston University

Married and the mother of three children

Job Experience

Assistant Director, Division of Disability Adjudication, Massachusetts Rehabilitation Commission, Boston, Mass., 1960–1974

Program Operations Analyst, Social Security Administration, Department of Health, Education and Welfare, Boston, Mass., 1974–1975

Description of Experience

During my fourteen-year tenure with the Division of Disability Adjudication I progressed from a disability specialist to the assistant director. As such I had the overall responsibility for the performance of the entire Division, which consisted of a staff of over 200 professional and clerical personnel. Funding for operation of the Division was entirely federal. Budget for 1974 was in excess of $4 million. As key administrative person in the Division I was responsible for the fiscal as well as the personnel side of the operation.

In 1974 the Social Security Administration offered me a position with the government assisting adjudication agencies in the other New England states to develop strong management techniques to meet the needs of rapid growth as the national disability program expanded.

Although I was successful in my years of work with the government and could anticipate further career advancement, I decided to resign in favor of operating my own business in the community in which I live.

Resumé

Robert J. Keefe
Greens Point Road
Ipswich, Mass. 01938

Married
Three Children

Education

Boston Public Schools
Brown University—A.B.
Boston State College—M.Ed.
Boston University and Harvard University—Credits

Work Experience

Cost Accountant—USAF, 1951–1953
English Instructor—Samsun College, Turkey, 1958–1960
Ass't Manager—Contemporary Designs, Brookline, Mass., 1960
English Instructor—Medford High School, Medford, Mass., 1961–1966
Department Chairman, English—Ipswich Public Schools, 1966–present

Business-Related Experience

Supervising 10–15 teachers and 700–1000 students in English courses in Ipswich

Budgeting, ordering and inventorying all materials and equipment for the above

Semester of Accounting at Northeastern University Night School

Three years' bookkeeping at various Air Force Bases

Three months' experience as assistant manager of a furniture store.

A two-page personal statement showed the Keefes' assets and liabilities:

PERSONAL STATEMENT

NAME   Joan and Robert Keefe
POSITION OR OCCUPATION   Chairman English Department, Ipswich H.S.
BUSINESS ADDRESS   Ipswich School System
RESIDENCE ADDRESS   Greens Point Road, Ipswich, Mass.

The following is submitted for the purpose of procuring, establishing and maintaining credit with you in behalf of the undersigned or persons, firms or corporations in whose behalf the undersigned may either severally or jointly with others execute a guaranty in your favor. The undersigned warrants that this financial statement is true and correct and that you may consider this statement as continuing to be true and correct until a written notice of a change is given to you by the undersigned.

DATE   August 23, 1975

Assets	In Even Dollars	Liabilities	In E⟨ Doll⟨
Cash on hand and in banks	8,525	Notes payable to banks—secured	
Marketable Securities—see Schedule A	225	Notes payable to banks—unsecured	17
Non-Marketable Securities—see Schedule B		Due to brokers	
Securities held by broker in margin accounts		Amounts payable to others—secured	
Restricted or control stocks		Amounts payable to others—unsecured	
Partial Interest in Real Estate Equities—see Schedule C		Accounts and bills due	5(
		Unpaid income tax	
Real Estate Owned—see Schedule D	50,000	Other unpaid taxes and interest	
Loans Receivable		Real estate mortgages payable—see Schedule D	33,7(
Automobiles and other personal property	21,800	Other debts—itemize	
		Master Charge	9(
Cash value—life insurance—see Schedule E		Harbor Master	34
Other assets—itemize	9,000		
Joint savings acct with mother Middlesex Institute for Savings			
		TOTAL LIABILITIES	35,6〕
		NET WORTH	53,9〔
TOTAL ASSETS	89,550	TOTAL LIAB. AND NET WORTH	89,5〔

Annual Sources of Income		Personal Information
Salary, bonus & commissions	18,000	Do you have a will? no If yes, name of executor.
Dividends		
Real estate income		Are you a partner or officer in any other venture? no
Other income		
		Married yes Minor children
		Single Other dependent
TOTAL		Age 43

Contingent Liabilities		General Information
Do you have any contingent liabilities? no		Are any assets pledged? no
If yes, give details:		Are you defendant in any suits or legal actions? no
As endorser, co-maker or guarantor	$	Personal bank accounts carried at Harbor Nat'l Ipswich Coop Mt. Vernon Coop.
On leases or contracts	$	
Legal claims	$	Have you ever taken bankruptcy? Explain.
Other special debt	$	
Amount of contested income tax liens	$	no

(COMPLETE SCHEDULES AND SIGN ON RE-VERSE SIDE)

Confidential

Schedule A — U.S. Governments and Marketable Securities

No. of Shares or Face Value (Bonds)	Description	In Name Of	Market Value
10	series E savings	Joan Keefe	225.

Schedule B—Non-Marketable Securities

Description of Securities	No. of Shares Owned	Book Value Per Financial Statement Dated:	No. of Shares Outstanding	Total Value

Schedule C—Partial Interests in Real Estate Equities

Location of Property	% of Ownership	Type	Yr. of Purch.	Cost (C) or Market (M)	Mortgage	Value of Equity

Schedule D—Real Estate Owned

Description of Property and Improvements	Date Acquired	Title in Name of	Cost	Market Value	Mortgage	
					Amount	Maturity
residence and 2½ Acres land Ipswich, Mass.	1972	Robert & Joan Keefe	37,500	50,000	34,700	25 yrs

Schedule E—Life Insurance Carried, Incl. N.S.L.I. and Group Insurance

Face Amount	Name of Company	Beneficiary	Cash Surrender Value	Loan
7,000	NSLI	Joan Keefe		
20,000	Group Insurance	Robert Keefe		

Schedule F—Names of Banks or Finance Companies Where Credit Has Been Obtained

Name	Date	High Credit	Owe Currently	Secured or
New England Merchants	1970	3000	paid	Unsecured
So. Shore National	1970	3000	paid	unsecured
Bay Bank & Trust	1972	3200	175.88	unsecured
Master Charge New England Merchants	1974	1000	900.	unsecured
Harbor Nat'l Bank Harbor Master	1974	1000	340.	unsecured
Ipswich Savings Bank	1972	34,000	33,700	unsecured

THE UNDERSIGNED CERTIFIES THAT BOTH SIDES HEREOF AND
THE INFORMATION INSERTED THEREIN HAS BEEN CAREFULLY
READ AND IS TRUE, CORRECT AND COMPLETE.

SIGNATURE _____

_____19_____ SIGNATURE _____

DATE SIGNED
(USE ADDITIONAL SCHEDULES WHEN NECESSARY)

The personal details having been covered, the Keefes
then tackled projected gross sales per item. From their research with suppliers and other shops they were able to
figure out the possible turnovers for each category of merchandise they planned to carry. And they knew, again
drawing information from wholesalers and other shops,
that they wanted to open up with $10,000 worth of inven-
tory on their shelves. They estimated gross sales as follows:

Books (the largest category of inventory)

Inventory	$6,000.00	(This would be outright pur-chase before the shop ever opened.)
plus 40%	$2,400.00	(The percentage they plan-ned to mark each item up.)
TOTAL	$8,400.00	(They added the markup to the starting inventory figure to show what they thought they would gross on books for their first year.)
Turnover: 5 × per year		(Figure given them by Na-tional Bookseller's Associa-tion.)

TOTAL PROJECTED
BOOK SALES: $42,000.00 (Total inventory figure mul-
                          tiplied by number of times it
                          would turn over during one
                          year equals projected gross.)

Joan and Bob went through the four categories of merchandise the Shaker Tree would sell—books, records,
plants and furniture—and ended up with a projected-
gross-sales estimate of $90,000. The loan application page
looked like this:

PROJECTED GROSS SALES, 1976

Item		Turnovers	Total sales
Books Inventory	$6,000		
plus 40%	2,400		
	$8,400	(×5)	$42,000.00
Records			
Inventory	$2,400		
plus 50%	1,200		
	$3,600	(10)	36,000.00
Plants			
Inventory	$600		
plus 100%	600		
	$1,200	(6)	7,200.00
Shaker Furniture			
Inventory	$1,000		
plus 25%	250		
	$1,250	(3)	3,750.00
			$88,950.00
			(Rounded to $90,000)

The next part of the loan-application data was the projected statement of earnings for 1976, 1977 and 1978. This is the page that puts everything together to show what profits can be made given their gross sales, and then subtracting the cost of goods sold in order to get an idea of gross profit. Next, the estimated yearly operating expenses were subtracted from the gross profits to find out what the possible net profit might be:

PROJECTED STATEMENT OF EARNINGS, 1976 THROUGH 1978

Gross Sales	1976	1977	1978
	$90,000	$95,000	$100,000

Cost of Goods Sold

	1976	1977	1978
Beginning inventory	$10,000	$10,000	$15,000
Purchases	60,600	65,000	65,000
Goods available forsale	$70,600	$75,000	$80,000
Ending inventory	10,000	15,000	15,000
Cost of goods sold	$60,600	$60,000	$65,000

Gross Profit	$29,400	$35,000	$35,000

Operating Expenses

Rent @ $275 per month	$3,300
Interest	1000
Utilities @ $50 per month	600
Insurance	200
Postage (and/or transportation)	900
Dues	40

Reference books	70		
Telephone	500		
Miscellaneous (fees etc.)	200		
Salary	5,200		
Advertising	500		
	$12,510	$13,000	$13,000

Net Income $16,890 $22,000 $22,000

Cash available to:
  pay taxes
  pay notes payable
  pay accounts payable
  turn back into business
  increase salaries

The final page in the Shaker Tree loan application is the month-by-month projected sales analysis for one year. A lot of outside research went into this page, from the local Chamber of Commerce, the library, the booksellers' association, the wholesalers and the suppliers they had located. Basing their figures on data that showed how other businesses fluctuated month to month, the Keefes put together an estimate of how their shop might do, given normal business conditions:

PROJECTED SALES ANALYSIS, 1976

Month	% **Sales**	**Books**	**Records**	**Plants**	**Shaker**	**Total**
October	10	$4,230	$3,600	$720	$450	$9,000
November	10	4,230	3,600	720	450	9,000
December	25	10,575	9,000	1,800	1,125	22,500
January	12	5,076	4,320	864	540	10,800
February	5	2,115	1,800	360	225	4,500
March	5	2,115	1,800	360	225	4,500

April	7	2,961	2,520	540	315	6,300
May	6	2,538	2,160	432	270	5,400
June	5	2115	1,800	360	225	4,500
July	4	1,692	1,440	288	180	3,600
August	4	1,692	1,440	288	180	3,600
September	7	2,961	2,520	504	315	6,300
TOTALS	100%	$42,000	$36,000	$7,200	$3,750	$88,950
% OF INVENTORY		(47%)	(40%)	(8%)	(5%)	$90,000 (rounded off)

Finally the loan was granted, for $12,000, as we said, and the shop opened and is doing well. The Keefes, now in their third year of business, have revised surprisingly little of their original plan of operation. The plants turned out to be a much smaller part of the entire shop and are now de-emphasized. Toys are added in depth at Christmas and Easter, and the book section has been expanded. Crafts from the New Hampshire League of Craftsmen and from Berea, Kentucky, are sold along with the Shaker furniture reproductions which are available in kits as well as pre-assembled.

The availability of bank loans varies in different parts of the country and in different economic climates. If you apply for a bank loan and are turned down, be sure to ask the loan officer to go over your application with you and point out which parts brought the negative response. Loan officers process hundreds of applications each month, and they can size up your proposal quickly and give you the best advice available.

A nice backup is offered to the small-business person by the Small Business Administration's Loan Guarantee Program. If your loan application looks *almost* good enough to accept but just a trifle too risky for the local banks, they can send the application packet to the loan officers in your local S.B.A. office, asking them to review your proposal.

Each loan application referred to the S.B.A. is read by two loan officers. If one of the loan officers passes the application, the bank is notified that the S.B.A. will underwrite the major part of the loan. The loan is then granted to you through your local bank, with the S.B.A. acting as guarantor. Private individuals cannot apply direct to the S.B.A. for the Loan Guarantee Program; the only access is through the loan department of a bank.

Another program designed to help small-business people is that of the Office of Minority Business Enterprise (OMBE), established in 1969 as part of the U.S. Department of Commerce. Its goal is "to increase minority business ownership to enable minority citizens to compete for their fair share of business sales and profits."

There are 35 million minority citizens in the country today—17 percent of the total population. OMBE statistics show that the minorities own only 4 percent of all businesses and account for less than 1 percent of all business receipts. To combat this, OMBE has developed multiple programs administered through a nationwide network of local offices.

By visiting one of the local OMBE offices, a minority person can get help on such diverse matters as developing a marketing plan, finding financing and setting up and maintaining an adequate cash flow. (See the Appendix for the addresses of the OMBE offices.)

5

Getting Organized

There are three ways to set up a business in the United States: individual proprietorship, partnership and incorporation. Each structure has its good and bad points, and each has a number of variations on the main theme. Most businesses go through at least two types of organization during their business life.

The individual proprietorship is the simplest form of business structure and the one most people begin with. It requires no lawyer and begins and ends at the will of the owner. When you set up an individual proprietorship, you let the rest of the world know that you are in business: it is a statement of your intention to carry on some type of business activity. If you decide to go out of business as an individual proprietor, you merely tell people you've stopped, and that ends that.

If you plan to conduct business under a made-up name—The Cinnamon Tree, The Golden Door, etc.—most states require you to register the name so they can track you down if the need arises. In some cases this registration form—the 'D.B.A.,' or 'Doing Business As,' form—is filed with your local county clerk's office, and in some cases with the State Department of Taxation.

Also, your bank will need a federal employer-identification number in order to set up your business bank account. Simply give them your social security number if you are an individual, or file Form SS-4, which can be had for the asking from the I.R.S. The form states your name, your address and information about your proposed business.

A major advantage to individual proprietorship is being able to run your own show at your own pace, as you see fit. This can also be one of the major disadvantages if you are too inexperienced, inept or reluctant to keep it going solo. How well you operate as an independent often comes down to how well you make decisions and accept responsibilities.

The big disadvantage to being an individual proprietor is that the owner is *personally liable* for all business debts, no matter how innocently incurred. For example, if any legal judgments are won against your business, all your personal property can be seized to pay the debts. This includes real estate, automobiles and an appalling list of life's little comforts.

Lawyers occasionally advise new business people considering individual proprietorships to divest themselves of major holdings as a protective measure. Taking your name off the deed to your house might make a lot of sense while you are testing out your business abilities. However, Milton Maybruck, my long-time friend/lawyer/accountant, cautions:

"The legal fees and expenses of trying to make yourself 'judgment proof' are usually more than the cost of incorporating. Remember also that if you do own any property and want it taken out of your name to protect it from creditors, you will have to put it into someone else's name. This can be risky, because relationships frequently change and/or deteriorate. You may have more problems with your 'nominee' than with your creditors."

The tax structure for an individual proprietorship is simple. Business profits are taxed as personal income, so you would be liable for federal and state personal income taxes the same as if you were on a straight salary.

As a self-employed person you still have to pay federal social security tax, although you will not need workmen's compensation and disability insurance, because you are considered an owner rather than a worker. In addition, many states, including New York State, levy a state income tax on profits from unincorporated businesses.

The second way to set up a business is the partnership—an arrangement made by two or more persons to operate a business together. It can be set up the same way an individual proprietorship is—by word of mouth—and can be ended in like manner. It also can be handled by having a lawyer draw up a partnership agreement outlining the relationships of all partners and specifying how and when the partnership may be dissolved.

However, some states require partnerships to file a Certificate of Conducting Business as Partners either with the local county clerk's office or with the state, identifying each and every partner. And if the partnership plans to do business under an assumed name, a 'D.B.A.' form will need to be filed in states requiring it.

The advantages of a partnership are obvious: two heads are often better than one. The disadvantages are equally obvious: partnerships are as tricky as marriages. Personal behavior patterns can get in the way, odd dependencies can develop, and old troubles can be acted out. Think many times before you take on partners.

The hazards of partnerships become magnified in light of the fact that each partner is personally liable for the *total amount* of business activity and business debt that the organization has. For example, if you are in a partnership of four people, each of you is liable *not* for one-fourth of everything, but for 100 percent of everything if the business does not pay its liabilities. So pick your partners carefully and set up good lines of communication from the beginning.

The tax situation of partnerships is similar to that of the individual proprietor. Each partner's share of the profits from the business will be taxed as personal income. In states having a tax on unincorporated businesses, profits from the business would also be taxed.

An interesting variation on the partnership is the limited partnership. In this, one "general partner" is designated to run the business, and all the other partners have a limited role, acting solely as investors, with no day-to-day input and no services rendered. Limited partnerships are commonly used to finance Broadway shows and large sporting events, real estate, etc.

Some states require the filing of a Certificate of Limited Partnership and a D.B.A. if the name is fictitious. A few states also want the D.B.A. notice to be published in whichever newspapers are designated by the county clerk.

The limited partners, aside from having a restricted role in the business, have limited liability up to the amount of money they invested (provided a properly drawn legal agreement protects the limited partners). Thus a limited partnership is more attractive to nonparticipant investors than a regular partnership, where each person is responsible for the actions and debts of the entire group.

The profits of a limited partnership are taxed the same as in a general partnership—as individual income. The limited partnership agreement is very technical and complex and must be set up by an attorney and filed with the state in accordance with each state's tax rules. Thus an attorney's fees and, in some states, a filing fee are added expenses.

Partnerships, be they general or limited, create rather intimate relationships during the life of the business. A common practice is to have each partner covered by life insurance payable to the surviving partners, to be used specifically to buy out the deceased's family. This guarantees immediate cash to the family and also ensures that the business operation will continue without interruption.

The third way to go into business is to set up a corporation and let the corporation do business by hiring you to carry out its activities. A corporation is, in a sense, an artificial person created under state law. It can be owned entirely by you or divided among a group, each of whom would buy and own shares of the corporation's capital stock. It can hire, fire, buy and sell, in accordance with the laws of whichever state it is incorporated in. Its birth certificate is called a "charter" and is best set up by attorneys familiar with the legal complexities. Most states do allow incorporation papers to be filed by nonattorneys, but the time and effort required to study all the possibilities hardly seems worth it when compared with legal fees of $250 to $400, currently the price range for incorporation.

The major attraction of a corporation is the protection it offers to the business person. Since the corporation—the artificial person—is the one doing business, all responsibilities are assumed by the corporation, and only properties owned by the corporation are liable in case of disaster. If, for example, you set up a corporation and the corporation buys a car, a building, shop fixtures, etc., all these possessions can be used to repay debts. However, your own home, car, yacht or whatever is protected, since it is owned by you and not by the corporation.

The exception is when the corporation has collected payroll or other taxes for the federal, state or local governments. These taxes generally constitute trust funds, and corporate officers can be held *personally* liable for the company's failure to pay them over.

A corporation might be a one-person business or a group, each owning shares of corporation stock. Stockholders may actively participate in the business or just put money in; there are no restrictions. Each state's laws do spell out some ground rules of how the corporation must behave, and generally the corporation's name must be researched by the state so there is no duplication or confusingly similar name.

It is important that you ask the attorney setting up your corporation or the accountant hired to do the books to furnish you with a yearly calendar outlining all the responsibilities of the corporation, including filing dates for taxes. Post it somewhere prominent and use it to remind yourself of the required pattern of doing business. If you miss any important dates, the government won't care that your accountant forgot to tell you!

A corporation must pay taxes on the profits it makes at different rates than an individual does. These rates tax the corporation's net income, which is its income after paying out officers' salaries.

A corporation may be more expensive in terms of taxes, because after it pays its own corporate income tax on its net income, if it distributes the remaining net income to its owners (its shareholders), they will receive it as a dividend and pay a second personal income tax on that income.

An important exception to these taxes is the Subchapter S corporations set up by the Internal Revenue Service to aid small businesses. Any small-business corporation can qualify itself for Subchapter S status by filing appropriate forms with the I.R.S.

To qualify for Subchapter S corporation status a corporation must meet the following six requirements:

1. It must be a domestic corporation
2. It must not be a member of an affiliated group
3. It must have only one class of stock
4. It must not have more than ten shareholders
5. It must have only individuals or estates as shareholders
6. It must not have a nonresident alien as a shareholder

Under Subchapter S the tax structure is similar to that of a partnership, where each shareholder must report his or her pro rata share of corporate profits as part of personal income, or deduct corporate losses from personal income (with certain limitations). The liability protection is unchanged in Subchapter S, which is intended to help a tiny business avoid a heavy corporate tax burden.

Getting rid of a corporation is almost as complicated as setting one up and is best left to lawyers and accountants. It can be sold through stock transfers, can go bankrupt or can be put to sleep quietly, but any method of termination is structured by law and must be adhered to.

Another variation on the three standard types of business organization is the cooperative, which straddles partnership and corporation. Cooperatives, though in today's news, are time-honored structures dating back to 1844, when twenty-eight flannel weavers in Rochdale, England, grouped together cooperatively to bypass an oppressive economic system. The co-op worked for them and it's working for more and more people each year.

American cooperatives are usually associated with agriculture and, in recent years, housing cooperatives. Some of the farmers' cooperatives of past decades have developed into the giants of the food world, helped by close liaison with the U.S. Department of Agriculture's Farmer Cooperative Service.

Cooperatives differ from other types of business organizations in three fundamental areas. Gerald Ely, author of the U.S.D.A. Economic Statistics & Cooperative Service booklet *The Cooperative Approach to Crafts*, defines these areas:

1. Service at Cost—This means that the cooperative does not make money for itself. Net margins above the cost of providing services belong to members of the cooperative in proportion to their patronage, resource contribution, labor, or according to some other predetermined basis for allocation.
2. Democratic Control—The association is controlled on some basis other than the amount of capital contributed. Generally this basis for control is one member–one vote.
3. Limited Return on Equity Capital—The return on capital invested in the cooperative is not the principal benefit sought by members as is the case with stockholders in a non-cooperative corporation.

Cooperatives are created by a group of people having a common economic or physical need. Retailing or marketing cooperatives are most often set up by designers and artisans producing the items they hope to sell. The activities of the cooperative are handled in the manner of a corporate business, but the group may or may not be legally incorporated. Some states have laws covering the incorporation of cooperatives; some cooperatives incorporate under the District of Columbia Cooperative Law and then incorporate in their own states as an out-of-state corporation.

When the group chooses legal incorporation, the liability protection shields the members just as in any corporation, and taxes on profits are paid by the corporation. When the group is not legally incorporated, it is viewed as a partnership with extended liabilities for all members, and the profits are taxed as individual income.

The management of a cooperative consists of general members, board of directors and hired management.

General members join the cooperative by purchasing shares of stock (also called membership shares). Democratic control is maintained by issuing every member one vote regardless of the extent of his or her stock purchase. The members elect a small board of directors, who oversee the actual operation. The board of directors usually hires a professional manager to carry out the day-to-day activities. Studies of cooperatives show that the success of the venture often depends on the ability and experience of the hired manager.

The major purpose of a retail-marketing cooperative is to provide an economic service for the members—that of displaying and selling merchandise more efficiently and more directly so higher profits can be realized by the producers. Thus the stockholders cannot look for the traditional promise of profit inherent in the purchase of conventional corporate stock.

When extra money does accrue to a cooperative, it is returned to the members through refunds in proportion to the activity of the individual member. For example, a refund system in a retailing cooperative might reflect the number of sales of each member's work, with those selling the most getting back a larger portion of the refunds than those with little selling activity. Refunds are taxable as personal income.

Disbanding a cooperative, if legally incorporated, should be done by a lawyer and an accountant. If the cooperative is not legally incorporated, it can be terminated in the same way a partnership is ended, i.e. by distributing the assets/liabilities equally among the members/partners, and then calling it quits.

The following comparison chart will clarify the characteristics of the different types of business organizations. It is reprinted from "Advising People About Cooperative," written by C. H. Kirkman, Jr. and Paul O. Mohn, and published by the Extension Service, Farmer Cooperative Service, U.S. Department of Agriculture.

METHODS OF DOING BUSINESS UNDER PRIVATE ENTERPRISE

A COMPARISON

Characteristics	Types of Business Enterprise			
			Corporate Form	
	Individual	Partnership	Investor-Oriented Corporation	User-Oriented Cooperative Corporation
Functions	To buy or produce goods for sale or provide service	Same as individual	Same as individual	To purchase supplies, market products or provide needed services
Objective	Profit for the individual	Profit for the partners	Profit for the investing stockholders	Profit for the members and patrons
Users	The public	The public	The public	Members and/or patrons
Ownership and Control	The individual	The partners	The investors	Members—usually one vote each[1]

Management	The indi- vidual	The partners	Board of Directors	Board of Di- rectors
Legal Status	Usually unincorporated	Legal agreement between associates under state law	Incorporated under state law	Usually in- corporated under specific state law
Liability	Assets of the indi- vidual	Assets of the partners	Assets of the corpo- ration	Assets of the cooperative
Return on Capital Invested	Unlimited	Unlimited	Unlimited	Limited by law[1]
Who Gets Net Proceeds?	The indi- vidual	The partners	The stockholders	The patrons in proportion to use[1]

[1]Distinctive cooperative characteristics

After you have selected the organizational structure you want, you need to acquire the necessary licenses and permits to do business in your area. Local, state and federal governments will be interested in your debut as a shop owner. However, the state government is most directly concerned with retail/wholesale activities, since these furnish most states with a large portion of their annual income. Once you clear yourself with your state tax bureau, you are well on the way to legitimacy and will find the added federal and local requirements to be minimal.

Each state has its own interpretation of revenue collecting. What they have in common is the need to keep track of all business activity, to protect the residents of the state and to make sure that any business that is making a profit sends some of that profit back to the government to support the expenses of the state. You might not agree with this system of taxation, but that's the way the country was set up, and if you want to get in the game, those are the rules.

It might be helpful to make a quick tour of the pertinent business tax structure so you can see where you fit in. The business that will concern you operates on two levels—wholesale and retail. On the wholesale level, the business owner purchases raw materials and changes or converts the raw materials into a product, which he or she then resells. In order to keep track of wholesale business activity, most states require the business owner to register with the state tax department and to receive, in turn, a registration number, which identifies him or her as a business person who is creating or purchasing items to re-sell.

Taxes are not normally levied on wholesale transactions. When the business person buys materials, he or she furnishes the registration number to the supplier. This is called "issuing a resale certificate." When the supplier receives the registration number or resale certificate, it is acknowledged as proof of the legitimacy of the purchaser's business status, and the supplier can furnish it to the state tax bureau to show why no taxes were collected as part of that sale of materials.

Many states have a form they suggest be used for issuing resale certificates. If your state has no preferred form, use the General Exemption Certificate form on page 209, in the Appendix.

On the retail level taxes are generally collected on all purchases made to be used personally by the purchaser. This is called the retail sales tax and is levied by the vast majority of states. In addition to state sales taxes, cities and/or counties may add on their own extra sales tax.

Who collects this retail sales tax? You, the shop or gallery owner, every time you sell something to a customer for personal use. If the customer wants to purchase something from you that she plans to resell, you must get a resale certificate or a copy of the customer's registration number so you can show why you didn't collect the retail sales tax from her. In effect you are acting as the representative of your state tax department, gathering up the taxes and sending them along, usually quarterly, to state tax headquarters.

So, step one for you, the prospective business owner, is to contact your state department of taxation and ask for information and applications to get your license or permit to operate a retail business. Remember, you can't do business legally without it. Some states give the licenses or permits out free, others charge something. For example, Delaware charges $50 for the first permit and then $10 for each branch store. Oklahoma has no charge. The state of Alaska charges $25 plus a percentage of your gross over a certain figure. Louisiana, on the other hand, charges a sliding scale based on your forecast of your gross receipts, which is then figured out on a table of charges determined by the state—e.g., $5 for under $5,000, etc.

A few states require a new shop owner to post a security bond for the first year or two. For example, Missouri wants a two-year bond or a cash deposit that covers three times the shop's average monthly tax liability. Nevada has a similar rule, stating the minimum bond or deposit to be $30, while the Texas bond or deposit must cover three times the quarterly tax liability, with a minimum of $25.

When you apply to your state tax department for a license or permit, you will receive detailed information about your responsibilities. If you have questions about any of it—forms or requirements—contact the nearest tax office and ask for clarification. It is vital for you to understand exactly what is expected of you.

If you collect sales or payroll or other taxes, keep the tax money separate, by opening a separate bank account for it. In practically all states, taxes collected are "trust monies" and you will be held personally responsible for them. Don't use them to finance your business operations; it could be the most expensive financing you ever receive. If you collect them, pay them.

Depending on your type of shop you might need additional permits or licenses. Food sale and service is generally monitored by state and local health departments and includes on-the-spot inspections. Zoning laws sometimes require specific sizes and types of exterior signs, marquees and banners, as do landmarks commissions if you locate in a historic area.

Life becomes slightly more complicated once you start hiring workers. You must obtain from the Federal Internal Revenue office an employer identification number. This is a simple form and merely reports preliminary information about the nature of the business in which you plan to be active. Ask for a copy of the *Employer's Tax Guide*, which will clue you in on what will be expected of you in reporting income tax withholdings, social security and federal unemployment tax.

Each state also has its own unemployment compensation laws that dovetail with the federal unemployment compensation laws, so you will need to contact your state department of labor, tell them what you're doing and ask how your business fits in with their requirements.

Having one or more full-time workers requires you to follow the U.S. Labor Department's standards on health and safety, which include displaying a poster that spells out the responsibilities of the employer, so include a request for that.

Workmen's compensation and disability insurance is required when you have a worker. Each state has its own version of compensation and disability, but all of them add up to guaranteeing each worker an income of sorts if he or she is injured while on the job (compensation) and also an income of sorts when he or she is ill or injured while off the job and therefore unable to work (disability). Data on these come from your state Workmen's Compensation and Disability boards.

Getting organized takes a lot of thinking and deciding, which is then followed by a lot of phoning and letter writing for applications and information about the responsibilities of a business owner. As the booklets come in, explaining each area, save them and use them as the beginnings of your personal business library.

Use the following checklist to make sure you've touched all bases:

Area Covered	Sent to	Answer Received
License/permit to do business	State Tax Department local office	
D.B.A. form	Local County Clerk's office or state Tax Bureau	
Certificate of Partnership or of Limited Partnership	County Clerk's office or state Tax Bureau	
Zoning regulations or landmarks specifications	County Clerk's office or Landmarks Commission local office	

License/permit for food sale or service	Local Health Department and state Health Department
Information on federal taxes; social security and unemployment; employer identification number	Federal Bureau of Internal Revenue local office
Information on state taxes and unemployment	Your state Tax Department local office
Health and safety requirements	U.S. Department of Labor local office
Workmen's Compensation	Your state Workmen's Compensation Board
Disability insurance	Your state Disability Office

6

Record Keeping

What the successful retailer needs most is not a better mousetrap—it's a simple system for keeping day-to-day records so she will know exactly where everything is. Up-to-date, understandable records bring serenity and peace of mind. No records, or incomplete ones, bring angst and a feeling of powerlessness, the likes of which go back to early childhood.

Happily, a wizard of a man has worked out a logical fill-in-the-blanks kind of system that any idiot can follow. Do it and you'll always know, each day, where you stand. The man is John De Young of the Minority Business Opportunity Program of the National Shoe Retailers Association. De Young's system was originally worked out for shoe sellers, but it functions well for any small retailing situation. It encompasses profit-and-loss sheets, unit control, "open to buy" and all those other phrases that belong to the world of retailing.

The system begins with the words HOT BRANDIE. An auspicious beginning, you might say. Underneath the letters you put corresponding numbers, to work out a secret code:

H	O	T		B	R	A	N	D	I	E
1	2	3		4	5	6	7	8	9	0

The code relates to the actual price you have *paid* for every item in your shop. Naturally, you will sell each thing for as much money as you feel you can get. Setting the retail prices is up to you. However, the cost of your stock is fixed by the manufacturers from whom you buy. It is this cost that you are interested in coding.

For example, an item you are retailing for $10 might have cost you $5. Translated into this code, your $10 item would have cost you:

R E E
(5.0 0)

Or you might be retailing something at $10 that you only paid $3.50 for. In code language this $10 item will have cost you:

T R E
(3.5 0)

You encode the actual price so your customers won't know what you paid for each purchase they make, but you will know, and be able to tally up at the end of each day.

One day you might sell ten items that retail for $10 but cost you $5 each, bringing your gross profit to $50. Another day you might sell ten items that cost you $3 apiece, so your profit per item would be $7, for a total of $70.

Both days show ten sales, but one brought you in $20 more

than the other. It's this actual cost—and *actual profit*—that you need to keep track of. It's easy to feel very busy and productive making lots of sales, but the real profit and the real cost are what count.

As your pre-opening inventory starts arriving, put the HOT BRANDIE code to work for you and place the corresponding code letters on each price tag, along with the selling information, such as price and size. A tag might look like this:

> Style # 7654
> Size: 8
> Price: $35.95
> HREE

This tag tells you that when you sell one size 8, style 7654, at $35.95, you paid $15 for it and thus have picked up $20.95 on the transaction. Of course, out of your $20.95 has got to come money to cover your overhead, etc., so you can't look at it as clear profit, or net profit. The $20.95 is gross profit, before expenses are deducted.

When you write up the sales slip for the above sale, you record the code letters along with the rest of the data:

SALES CHECK

Date: 4/5/77

#7654, Size 8, HREE	$35.95
Sales tax	1.80
TOTAL	$37.75

Before you open your shop be sure that each price tag is coded and that all sales help understand that they must record the letters on every sales slip. Without this information the system won't work.

The next step is setting up your first year's tally sheets— one per month. Make twelve copies of the following form, omitting the figures, set them up in a file folder and keep them handy for daily use. This is where you record all the information from the sales slips.

At the end of each business day take all that day's sales slips and transfer the pertinent information onto the tally sheets. On Sunday total up each column for that week. At the end of the month total up each column.

Each of the column entries is a vital part of the overall picture. The sales tax is the amount that must be paid to the state government. Keep it separate from other funds so that when the time arrives to send in your quarterly statement you'll have the money ready. Experience has shown that when the sales tax money is grouped in with other monies it has a habit of becoming lost.

The daily sales figure is important because it helps you understand and control one of your largest expenses—the payroll. Fifteen percent of the total volume any shop does is the best amount that shop should spend on payroll. At the end of each month multiply the daily sales total by 15 percent. The answer you get will tell you how much you can currently afford to spend on payroll. Increase or decrease the number of hours you employ sales help in proportion to what your percentages tell you.

The total cost-of-sales figure tells you what amount of money you have at your disposal at the end of the month to buy new merchandise to replace what has been sold. More on this "open-to-buy" later.

The gross profit column is the amount you've taken in *minus* the cost of sales. From this figure you will eventually subtract all your expenses. After the expenses (overhead) are deducted, the amount you have left is your net, or actual, profit for that month. If you find that after deducting expenses from the gross profit figure you have a deficit, this is the amount you are in the hole and will have to replace from other sources.

Apparel retailers generally show a loss for four months of the year. A common replacement practice is to "borrow" on paper enough money from your cost-of-sales total to bring you up to a break-even point. This simply means that you have less money to spend on new merchandise during the coming month to replace the stock that has been sold. Be judicious, and remember that replacement merchandise is necessary each and every month to keep the store functioning, looking up to date and offering regular customers tempting new treats.

The columns on the right-hand side of the double line are to be filled in as the expenses occur. In the expenses column make note of every check you write or every bit of cash you spend to keep the shop going.

The payroll for a small store is usually met once a week. As you pay out, enter the amount in the payroll column. At the end of each month add up all the expenses you've paid out plus the four weekly payrolls you have met.

To get a final tally that will tell you what condition your business is in, use the profit-or-loss column. Enter the gross-profit figure first. Below it put the amount of total expenses. Subtract expenses from gross profit. The figure you get will represent your net, or actual, profit—the "take-home" for you after the stock that's been sold has been replaced.

		Sales Tax	Daily Sales	Cost of Sales	Gross Profit	Profit or Loss	All Expenses		Daily	Payroll
W	1	3.18	100.32	61.18	39.14		Rent		800.00	
Th	2	4.19	218.96	108.91	110.05		Loan		218.00	
F	3	6.27	286.19	150.01	136.18		Interest		119.01	
S	4	10.44	491.91	250.90	241.01		Payroll			200.00
S	5	➤24.08	➤1097.38	➤571.00	➤526.38					
M	6	3.91	152.52	80.02	72.50		Stamps		1.25	
T	7	3.62	140.40	70.01	70.39		Light bulb		3.18	
W	8	3.18	100.32	61.18	39.14		Adv.		118.00	
Th	9	4.19	218.96	108.91	110.05					
F	10	6.27	286.19	150.01	136.18					
S	11	10.44	491.91	250.90	241.01		Payroll			200.00
S	12	➤31.11	➤1390.30	➤721.03	➤669.27					
M	13	3.91	152.52	80.02	72.50		Repair gate		76.01	
T	14	3.62	140.40	70.01	70.39		Insurance		200.00	
W	15	3.18	100.32	61.18	39.14		Travel		100.00	
Th	16	4.19	218.96	108.91	110.05		Phone		80.00	
F	17	6.27	286.19	150.01	136.18					
S	18	10.44	491.91	250.90	241.01		Payroll			200.00
S	19	➤31.11	➤1390.31	➤721.03	➤669.27					
M	20	3.91	152.52	80.02	72.50					
T	21	3.62	140.40	70.01	70.39					
W	22	3.18	100.32	61.18	39.14					
Th	23	4.19	218.96	108.91	110.05					
F	24	6.27	286.19	150.01	136.18					
S	25	10.44	491.91	250.90	241.01		Payroll			200.00
S	26	➤31.11	➤1390.31	➤721.03	➤669.27	GROSS-	2962.45			
M	27	3.41	152.52	80.02	72.50	EXPS.-	2515.45			
T	28	3.62	140.40	70.01	70.39	NET	447.00			
W	29	3.18	100.32	61.18	39.14	PROFIT				
Th	30	4.19	218.96	108.91	110.05					
F	31	6.27	286.19	150.01	136.18					
		➤20.67	➤898.39	➤470.13	➤428.26					
		138.08	6166.67	3204.22	2962.46				1715.45	800.00
			.15						+ 800.00	
TOTAL			925.01						2515.45	

If the net profit doesn't suit you, go back over all the expenses and cost of sales and see where you can adjust things for the future. Changes might include finding new, less expensive resources for some of your inventory, increasing your markup, cutting down on travel or staying off the telephone.

As long as you will in the blanks faithfully each day and do the weekly and monthly tallies, you will always know what your financial condition is and will be able to base your plans on fact. At the end of the first year review the twelve tally sheets to get an idea of the flow of business activity, the need for extra sales help and how your publicity-and-promotion schedule actually affected your profits. (See Chapter 10.)

The second half of John De Young's records system spins off the figures you get in the cost-of-sales column. The monthly cost-of-sales totals tell you how much money you can spend on goods to replace what has been sold—*after* you adjust them, if you have to, to help make up for any monthly deficit. The need to stay within this figure cannot be emphasized too strongly. To maintain a tight rein on spending, duplicate the following form twelve times, one for each month, excluding the sample figures and substituting your own.

ON-ORDER RECORD

Month: August   **Open to receive: $950.00**

Order Number	Date Due	Name of Manufacturer	Style	Quan.
412	10/12	ABC	21516	120
413	10/16	XYZ	100	150
414	10/16	PED	7480	110
415	11/12	OPT	3210	180
416	11/19	ABC	4700	72
417	11/26	POD	712	96
418	12/2	XYZ	142	150
419	12/2	TOL	2160	72
			TOTAL	950

On the first business day of each month transfer the figure of the total cost of sales of the previous month off your monthly tally sheet and onto the open-to-receive space. This is the retailer's phrase for the total amount of money available to be spent on new merchandise, i.e. the amount your books show you are "open to receive" in stock. You need not spend every penny, but you should not spend more than the given amount.

Each time you place an order, enter the information on this form. Be specific describing the order, and include shipping charges if you expect to pay for them. Total up what you have spent each time you enter an order. When the amount that you have spent equals the amount you have open to receive for that month—stop. You're done for the month and should not make any purchases until next month.

If you faithfully follow both the monthly tally sheets and the open-to-receive form, you will know where your business is day by day.

Markdowns, an essential part of retailing, figure into the monthly tally sheets and change the entire profit picture. Markdowns are normal and necessary to reduce inventory and to free your cash for new purchases. Warehousing unsold stock, whether on your shelves or packed away until the following season, deprives you of the use of your own cash. The longer you hold old merchandise, the more it costs you in storage and in opportunities lost for great new buys. Also, old merchandise has a way of looking weary. Plan on periodic markdowns to clean house.

There are two traditional markdown periods during the year, both keyed to climate and living changes. The first one begins immediately after Christmas and extends into February, with some special one-day sales on Lincoln's or Washington's birthday. Items and clothing tied into winter living are cleared away, creating money and space for new warm-weather replacements.

The second traditional markdown period is in August,

getting rid of warm-weather and vacation merchandise and making room for fall and back-to-school items.

Many stores use a three-phase markdown system, taking a certain amount off when the sale first breaks, then, a week or so later, taking another price cut, and finally, for the end of the sale period, cutting prices sharply on whatever is left. However, it doesn't take long for regular customers to figure this method out and to wait at least until the second markdown is made before they buy.

Some shops begin their sale with markdowns only on merchandise that has sold the least. Then, as the sale period progreesses, they add some of the more popular stock, also marked down. If the more popular merchandise isn't sold during the sale weeks, it is returned to stock at the pre-sale prices.

A "no sales ever" policy is held by some high-fashion boutiques. Here it is more important to the retailer to maintain a fashion authority image than to soften their mistakes through markdowns.

Obviously, the more skillful your buying is, the fewer markdowns you will have. Too many markdowns forecast disaster unless there is a change in your purchasing habits. But how many is too many? There is no one formula. John De Young cautions that shoe retailers run into trouble if their markdowns exceed 8 percent of their total yearly sales. Other fields have other ratios.

Until you have some idea of your markdown pattern—and every store has one—consider raising your initial markup a small percentage to cover contingencies. You can adjust the extra markup periodically and phase it out when you no longer need that kind of cushion.

Monitor your markdowns carefully to see if you can detect a pattern in the unprofitable buying. Try to figure out why each markdown didn't sell the way you thought it would. Successive markdowns in any one category of merchandise might be telling you that the market demand for the item is too small to bother with and you should stop carrying it.

Getting rid of the sale leftovers can be handled many ways. Donations to charities, schools, hospitals, etc. give you some tax write-offs, and some brownie points in heaven. Large cities generally have an active network of job-lot companies that purchase leftovers in quantity. Fabric and fabric scraps get sold to rag dealers, usually by the pound. Explore your area for possibilities.

In addition to keeping up the two monthly record pages—the tally sheet and the open-to-receive form—you will be aiming toward a yearly balance sheet and a yearly profit-and-loss statement. Both of these are summaries of the past year and generally cover from January 1 through December 31.

It is possible to do your own balance sheet and profit-and-loss statement, but the savings in time, effort and worry are vast when you have an accountant do them. But plan to work *with* the accountant so you can have an understanding of the sum totals for your store.

The balance sheet is a close-up of the condition the business is in as of December 31 of the year. It covers:

Assets

This means what your business owns. Your possessions are divided into "current assets" and "fixed assets." The current ones include cash, inventory and any money anybody owes you—your accounts receivable. The fixed assets are everything you have that helps you do business but that will not be sold or used up—fixtures, furniture, truck, insurance, etc.

Liabilities   This means what your business owes. It includes merchandise you have ordered and not yet paid for, bank loans, notes, mortgages, etc.

Capital   What the business is worth. Capital is the difference between all your assets and all your liabilities. Deduct what you owe from what you own and there you have it—your shop's capital worth. This total is sometimes called "net worth," "equity" or "proprietorship."

Ask your accountant to go over the completed balance sheet and help you interpret it into information you can use. For example, in some businesses a ratio of two-to-one is desired—that your assets be large enough to cover your liabilities *twice*. Other businesses have other ratios that indicate financial health. The balance sheet tells a lot about any business, which is why it is among the first items asked for when you apply for a bank loan.

The profit-and-loss statement is a short history of what has occurred during the course of the past year. It tells your gross profit and your yearly expenses and ends up with that all-important bottom line—the net profit.

Most of this you and your accountant will take from the monthly tally sheets. Your income tax return is almost totally derived from the profit-and-loss statement. It will be of interest to the bank loan officer as a counterpart to the balance sheet.

To clarify record keeping for the small business owner, the U.S. Small Business Administration has worked out the following calendar:

Small Business Financial Status Checklist
(What an Owner-Manager Should Know)

Daily
1. Cash on hand.
2. Bank balance (keep business and personal funds separate).
3. Daily Summary of sales and cash receipts.
4. That all errors in recording collections on accounts are corrected.
5. That a record of all monies paid out, by cash or check, is maintained.

Weekly
1. Accounts Receivable (take action on slow payers).
2. Accounts Payable (take advantage of discounts).
3. Payroll (records should include name and address of employee, social security number, number of exemptions, date ending the pay period, hours worked, rate of pay, total wages, deductions, net pay, check number).
4. Taxes and reports to State and Federal Government (sales, withholding, social security, etc.).

Monthly
1. That monthly records are complete. This shows assets (what the business has), liabilities (what the business owes), and the investment of the owner.
2. The Bank Statement is reconciled. (That is, the owner's books are in agreement with the bank's record of the cash balance.)
3. The Petty Cash Account is in balance.

(The actual cash in the Petty Cash Box plus the total of the paid-out slips that have not been charged to expense total the amount set aside as petty cash.)

4. That all Federal Tax Deposits, Withheld Income and FICA Taxes (Form 501) and State Taxes are made.
5. That Accounts Receivable are aged, i.e., 30, 60, 90 days, etc., past due. (Work all bad and slow accounts.)
6. That Inventory Control is worked to remove dead stock and order new stock. (What moves slowly? Reduce. What moves fast? Increase.)

7

Taxes

As you have gathered from the last chapter, taxes are all-encompassing, can be confusing, and are about to become a major factor in your life. Knowing your tax situation is important on two counts. First, it prevents you from falling behind on filing any of the myriad forms and payments, second, an understanding enables you to plan a more profitable future for your business. If you know the tax advantages and deductions available to you, it is possible to schedule your operation to qualify and thus end up with less taxable income, which means more money for you.

Sound a bit shady? Set your mind at ease. A much quoted explanation by the late Judge Learned Hand sums it all up: "Over and over again courts have said that there is nothing sinister in arranging one's affairs to keep taxes as low as possible. Everybody does so, rich or poor; and all do right, for nobody owes any public duty to pay more than the law demands."

When you operate your own business your tax responsibilities fall into two areas. In one role you are a person who owes taxes to the state, federal and/or local governments. An example of this is the local real estate tax you will pay if you own your own building. Another example is the income tax you pay to the federal government, whether you work for yourself, your own corporation, or others.

The second role you play is that of an agent doing a job for each of the tax departments. When you make a sale in your shop you are expected to collect your state's sales tax money, and forward it to the proper agency at the right time. And when you make out your payroll you are expected to deduct various amounts of money from your employees' pay to cover such things as Social Security and income taxes. In some cases you will merely hold the deducted amounts and then pass them on to the appropriate tax department. In other cases you will be expected to add some of your own money as the employer's contribution, and then pass the total sum on to the proper agency.

A fine preparation for your dual role as a small business owner is to set up your banking so that your business and personal monies never become confused with the funds you collect while acting as a tax agent. This generally involves three separate bank accounts: one for your tax monies, one for your shop and one for your personal or family life.

Monitor the relationship between the three accounts very carefully and be sure that the three stay eternally separate. As soon as tax monies are collected or set aside, hurry them into the proper account before they become dissipated on current expenses. When and if the business bank account runs short, grant a loan from the personal account—on paper, including a schedule for repaying the money. You might feel a little ridiculous writing up a loan to yourself, but it's a no-fail way to keep accounts straight and know exactly what your financial picture is at any given moment.

C.P.A. Reva Calesky, Director of Feminist Financial Consultants, New York City, advises new business owners to ". . . act as if your money belongs to somebody else. Keep careful track of it and be ready to account for it the same way you would be if your boss asked you to."

Past experience has proven to her that the most common tax problem new business owners have is learning to keep adequate records so they know the financial health of their business and can document legitimate expenses for tax deductions. Sole proprietors are the worst offenders. They have the most difficulty separating their *Person* from their *Business*. Too often it all runs together. Eventually the businessperson becomes discouraged at never seeming to make/have any money but is unable to figure out exactly what went wrong or what can be changed.

Ms. Calesky recommends that new business people have an initial consultation with an accountant during their pre-opening planning period. In the operation of your business you will have to cope with tax requirements from the Internal Revenue Service, your own state's tax department and most probably your local tax agency. By diligently studying the free literature available, you could pull together an idea of what each of the three expect from you. However, a one hour session with a good accountant will swiftly organize your responsibilities and alert you to future advantages for advance planning. Accountant's fees vary across the United States, but $50.00 for the initial consultation is average.

Business owners begin their tax thinking when they establish their fiscal year, also referred to as a tax year. A calendar year is twelve consecutive months ending on December 31st. A fiscal year is twelve consecutive months ending on the last day of any month other than December. Retailers generally establish their fiscal year so that it will fall in their least busy month. Reva Calesky thinks that often fiscal years are set up at the convenience of the accountant, avoiding the harried pre-income tax months of February, March and April.

Sole proprietors do not have the privilege of selecting a fiscal year because the profits and/or losses for their business are reported as part of their regular calendar year income tax return due on April 15th. As the business grows and becomes incorporated, a fiscal year may be established that differs from the calendar year. Also, if a corporation or legal partnership wishes to change its fiscal year to a more advantageous date, application may be made to the IRS showing that there is a substantial business purpose for the change and that the tax advantage resulting from it will not be significant.

Establishing the fiscal year is important to the business owner because the due date for filing the corporate tax return is the fifteenth day of the third month after the close of the fiscal year. For example, if your fiscal year ended in March, your corporate tax would have to be filed by June 15th, several months after your personal income tax filing date.

When approaching taxes it helps to understand the difference between deductions and tax credits and to develop an overview of how the system is put together. Deductions refer to all the costs you incur in order to sell your goods and run your business. Tax credits, on the other hand, are little rewards you may get for doing certain things. An example of a tax credit of interest to small businesses is the Tax Reduction and Simplification Act of 1977 which created a Jobs Tax Credit to provide employers with a tax incentive to create new jobs. If you added people to your staff, even on a part-time basis, you may be able to get a tax credit.

The way it all hangs together is pretty simple. Every year, at the proper time, you add up all your income. Then you deduct the cost of goods sold (the IRS Tax Guide for Small Businesses tells what you need to know, and it's free from the IRS.) The figure you arrive at once you've deducted the cost of goods sold from your total income is called your gross profit. Then, from the gross profit figure you deduct expenses incurred in running your business, such as travel and entertainment, etc. Again, check the Guide. Once you've deducted the business expenses you have reached your taxable income. Then you deduct any tax credits you have gotten, subtracting them from your taxable income total.

The overview is simple, but the actual figuring is complex and should be done by and with your accountant. Many deductions can also be handled as tax credits, and vice versa. Your accountant will be able to decide which will benefit you more.

One of the first things a new business owner must do is apply for a Taxpayers Identification Number, also called Employers Identification Number. The application must be made on forms available at all IRS offices. Your identification number must be shown on all business documents, and is often printed on the business checks from your bank. Sole proprietors in some areas can use their Social Security number on their income tax return and declaration of estimated taxes, but most parts of the country require an identification number. Check with your banker.

The federal taxes most people know about are the income and the Social Security taxes. Less known but equally important are federal unemployment tax and excise taxes.

The amount of federal income tax you must pay depends

on the manner in which your business is organized, your exemptions, deductions and credits, and whether or not you have any outside income.

For example, if you are an individual proprietor you pay your income tax just like everybody else. You file the same form as any citizen taxpayer. However, your main income comes from the profits of your shop rather than a salary you might get for working for somebody else. To clarify the shop profits as income, you include with your regular return an additional schedule which shows expenses and income from the business, documenting how you arrived at the tax you claim you owe. The extra forms are available at any IRS office.

A similar set of returns and extra, explanatory data must be filed by partnerships to document the income and expenses of the business. As a partner, you will report only your share of the profit on your individual tax return.

In addition, individual proprietors and partners are required to file a Declaration of Estimated Tax on or before April 15th of each year. The Declaration is an estimate of the income and the self-employment tax you expect to owe for the coming year, based on past records. Quarterly payments are made on the estimated amounts, with checks going to the IRS on April 15th, June 15th, September 15th and January 15th. If the estimate is inaccurate, adjustments are made at the time of payment.

If your business is organized as a Subchapter S corporation, its income will be taxed to the shareholders, that is, directly, in the same manner as in an individual proprietorship.

If your business is any other type of corporation, it will pay taxes on its corporate profits. In addition, you as owner-manager will pay income tax on the salary and dividends your corporation pays to you. Most corporations file yearly tax returns, but pay their taxes quarterly. Every corporation whose estimated tax is $40.00 or more is required to make estimated tax payments.

So much for your federal income taxes. As an employer you are expected to help your employees with their federal income taxes by withholding a certain amount of their wages and sending the money on to the IRS periodically. When you hire an employee you ask them to fill out a W-4 form stating the exemptions and additional withholding allowances he is claiming. By using the withholding tables furnished to you by the IRS you figure out the amount of money to withhold. Each December you ask every employee to make out a new W-4 form if there have been changes in their exemptions since the last time they filled one out. At the end of each year you make out a Wage and Tax statement, Form W-2, for each employee. The worker files one along with his own income tax return and you send along your duplicate copy to the IRS on or before February 28th.

Social Security taxes are handled in a similar manner. You deduct the tax from your employee's wages, add in a matching amount as the employer's contribution, and send it all along to the tax bureau at the appropriate time. The figures you will be dealing with change from year to year. In 1978, Social Security tax was only taken out of the first $17,700 the employee earned, and the amount you withhold and also match was 6.05% of that wage. IRS and Social Security Administration offices have the tables showing the amounts to withhold and to match for different wage levels.

Currently Congress is considering changes in the Social Security wage base, perhaps to equalize the amounts deducted from large and small wage earners. If anything comes out of the debate the IRS and Social Security Administration will have information for employers.

Federal excise taxes are imposed on the production, sale or consumption of certain commodities, not on the profits of your business. Items such as liquor, beer and firearms are subject to excise taxes. If you own and operate a truck in your business you have to pay federal highway use tax. The IRS will furnish you with complete information about taxable items and circumstances. If you are liable for any of these taxes you must file a quarterly return and make monthly or semi-monthly deposits. In the filing and paying of excise taxes, as with other taxes, it is your responsibility as a businessperson to figure out whether or not the tax applies to you and how much and when it must be paid.

The final category of federal tax that involves most small businesses is the unemployment tax. The involvement occurs if you pay wages of $1,500 or more in any calendar quarter, or if you have one or more employees on at least some portion of one day in each of twenty or more calendar weeks. The unemployment tax is levied on you the employer; it cannot be collected or deducted from the salaries of your workers.

To facilitate this, every employer utilizes the employer identification number on all documents and returns.

Questions on the status of part-time and free-lance people often come up. A full explanation is available in the Tax Guide for Small Businesses which states: "Under common law rules, every individual who performs services subject to the will and control of an employer, both as to what shall be done and how it shall be done, is an employee". . . and adds, ". . . the employee also means any individual who performs services for remuneration under the following conditions: . . as homeworkers performing work according to specifications furnished by the persons for whom the services are performed, on materials or goods furnished by such persons and required to be returned to them or to persons designated by them."

If you find you should be paying federal unemployment tax, currently the basic tax rate is 3.2% of the first $4,200 of taxable wage paid to the worker. However, the federal government allows you credit for the unemployment taxes you pay to your state government, so the actual sums of money may well be less than 3.2%.

This brings us to the state taxes for which you are responsible. There are only three main categories of state taxes: income, unemployment and sales taxes.

Not all states have income taxes. When they do, business owners are expected to deduct the tax from their employees' salaries. Some states use filing forms similar to the federal; other states ask you to fill out a different type of information sheet. It is important that you request data from your state tax agency and understand your responsibilities.

Every state has some form of unemployment tax, most often paid in full by the employer, but in a few cases assisted by payroll deductions from the worker's salary. The rate of tax varies from state to state but is usually based on the taxable wage base of a quarter. Again, contact your state tax agency for information.

If your state has a sales tax you will be expected to collect it on every retail sale your shop makes, and forward it to the sales tax department of your state tax agency. The percentage of sales taxes vary widely so get details and forms from your state agency.

The final group of taxes you might be liable for are city, county or other local taxes. These sometimes include real estate or business occupancy taxes, personal property taxes and taxes on unincorporated businesses. Whatever they are in your area, you are responsible to understand and pay them.

All of this reinforces the suggestion made in the beginning of this chapter—find an accountant you feel you can work with, set up an initial consultation, work out a calendar schedule of your shop's tax obligations, post it in a prominent place and follow it to the letter.

To simplify the calendar-making, the Small Business Administration has designed the following worksheet which they recommend you take to your accountant and use as a basis for your own schedule. Fill it in, stick to it, and feel confident you have demystified the bugaboo of taxes.

TAX OBLIGATIONS

Kind of Tax	Due Date	Amount Due	Pay to	Date for Writing the Check
FEDERAL TAXES				
Employee Income Tax and Social Security Tax	_____	_____	_____	_____
	_____	_____	_____	_____
	_____	_____	_____	_____
	_____	_____	_____	_____
Excise Tax	_____	_____	_____	_____
Owner-Manager's and/or Corporation's Income Tax	_____	_____	_____	_____
	_____	_____	_____	_____
	_____	_____	_____	_____
	_____	_____	_____	_____
Unemployment Tax	_____	_____	_____	_____
	_____	_____	_____	_____
	_____	_____	_____	_____
	_____	_____	_____	_____

STATE TAXES

Unemployment Taxes _____ _____ _____ _____
_____ _____ _____ _____
_____ _____ _____ _____
_____ _____ _____ _____

Income Taxes _____ _____ _____ _____

Sales Taxes _____ _____ _____ _____
_____ _____ _____ _____
_____ _____ _____ _____
_____ _____ _____ _____

Franchise Tax _____ _____ _____ _____

Other _____ _____ _____ _____
_____ _____ _____ _____
_____ _____ _____ _____
_____ _____ _____ _____

LOCAL TAXES

Sales Tax _____ _____ _____ _____
_____ _____ _____ _____
_____ _____ _____ _____
_____ _____ _____ _____

Real Estate Tax _____ _____ _____ _____

Personal Property Tax _____ _____ _____ _____

**Licenses (retail,
vending machine, etc.)** _____ _____ _____ _____

Other _____ _____ _____ _____
  _____ _____ _____ _____
  _____ _____ _____ _____
  _____ _____ _____ _____

8

Merchandise

If you are like most shop owners, months, perhaps years, of musing over the contents of your shop preceded the actual signing of the lease. You know pretty much what you want to include and how you want the shop to look on opening day. This chapter deals with getting it all together—out of your head and onto the shelves.

Locating the large manufacturers from whom you want to buy is relatively simple. Get the classified telephone directory from the nearest sizable city and check all pertinent listings, including "Manufacturers' Agents and Representatives," "Jobbers," and "Convertors." If local contacts are not satisfactory, write to the home offices of companies advertising in trade and consumer magazines and request that their road men contact you.

Attending regional markets is another way of gleaning resources. Whatever your field, there are trade shows given several times a year in many parts of the country designed to offer new merchandise to retailers. Trade papers and trade associations print notices and calendars of the shows well in advance. New York, Chicago, Dallas, Los Angeles, Kansas City, Atlanta, St. Louis and Boston all host trade shows in most categories of consumer goods and apparel.

You owe it to yourself to check the big markets at least once to find out what kinds of items are there. You may decide you never need to go again, but don't skip exploring them. The big markets are designed to present mass-produced products for mass marketing. Tiny specialty stores avoid this kind of thing on general principle, preferring to feature unique merchandise, but a trade show will add an understanding of your field that you can't get any other way. Attending markets is a bona fide business expense and is generally tax-deductible if no other stopovers are tacked on to the trip.

Once you have located resources and want to place an order, you must be prepared to document your validity. Carrying a copy of your resale number does this nicely, proving that your state government has recognized you as a business person entitled to make wholesale purchases. Business cards and/or business letterheads are also helpful.

Wholesale purchases are quantity purchases. Each category of merchandise has its selling increments—by the pair, the dozen, the gross, the pound, etc. Quantity discounts are standard; the more you buy, the more the price goes down per piece. The lure of quantity discounts is sometimes fatally tempting, so hold on to your true needs no matter what is offered.

When shopping the wholesalers, take care to coordinate the delivery dates of related items so you don't end up with pieces missing in your overall plan. Both apparel and home-fashion merchandising is very much a matter of presenting *total looks*. The end results are better for the consumer and will bring you more sales than if you promoted unrelated items. When placing orders, work from your coordinating possibilities rather than from each manufacturer's shipping schedules. If an item can't meet your deadline, replace it with something similar that has a better delivery date.

Plan to pay cash before delivery for the pre-opening merchandise. Credit in any field is hard to get, so don't waste time trying to set up deferred payment with your first-time suppliers. C.O.D. is the standard procedure with new accounts, protecting the supplier at the expense of the purchaser. Your cash is then tied up in merchandise and unavailable to you until sales are made.

Establishing credit with your wholesale suppliers will make your life a lot easier. Depending on the speed with which you reorder, ask for a line of credit as soon as you have given two or three orders. Unfortunately, wholesalers in most fields will want you to give them the names of other resources who have extended credit to you. As a newcomer you may find yourself stymied—no one will extend you credit until somebody else has. Eventually somebody gives in and takes a chance on you and the problem is solved, but expect to fight for your credit.

You will be asked for your bank references and perhaps a Dun & Bradstreet rating in addition to names of manufacturers who have given you credit. If your relationship with your personal banker is good, give the supplier his or her name so your reference will be as glowing as possible. Few new shop owners have access to Dun & Bradstreet or other credit information agencies, so pass gracefully on that one and refer back to your banker.

Once somebody agrees to go along and extend you credit it will come through in the form of "terms." These are the methods of payment used throughout the world of wholesaling:

Pro forma   When your order is ready for shipment you will be notified.

You then send part of the total payment, usually 50 percent. When your check is cleared through the bank, the supplier ships your order. Then you have 30 days in which to send the rest of the money.

2/10/net/30

Versions of this system are used much more often than pro forma invoicing. With this payment method you get a little reward if you pay the total bill early and are penalized if you pay later. 2/10 translates into you being able to deduct 2 percent off the total bill if you pay it within 10 days after receiving it. The net/30 part states that you must pay the entire amount within 30 days of the bill. The unwritten implication is, of course, that the seller will begin dunning you for the money after 30 days.

The figures can be changed around—e.g., 3/15/net/60, or any combination—but the reward system works out the same way.

30/60/90

This method is usually reserved for extra-large orders, to help tide you over until the money comes in. You pay one-third of the total bill within the first 30 days after receiving the shipment. Then you pay another third after 60 days, and the final

third 90 days after you receive
the merchandise. No early-pay
discounts are offered.

No one of these credit arrangements is the answer in all
fields. Again, as a new shop owner, take anything you can
get, because it frees up your own capital to use however
you want.

For the apparel and home-fashion fields, dealing
through resident buying offices or merchandise brokers is
a way around the credit maze, although one that costs you
extra money. It also brings you data on trends and market
coverage and helps place orders for you. They provide
credit in the following way:

Buying offices are set up to service shops with average
yearly gross over $50,000. The shop owner signs a con-
tract, normally for a year, paying a flat fee or a percentage fee based on how much business they do. Services
usually include:

- Market coverage information in the form of daily,
  weekly, bimonthly and monthly reports with sketches
  and photographs of best-selling items, new ideas, new
  product resources.
- Fashion and fabric information, sometimes with
  swatches.
- Promotional ideas and advertising aids, layouts and
  copy; sometimes a mat service is included. (See Chapter 9.)
- Supervising placing of orders for the out-of-town shop
  owner and complete follow-through on special orders.
- Consultations with individual store owners with rec-
  ommendations for the uses of the shop's open-to-buy
  funds.

- Fashion shows presenting total looks and coordinating suggestions, and/or store clinics.
- Aid in tracking down items a member store is seeking.
- Desk and phone space in the buying office for out-of-town shop owners who come to cover the markets themselves.

Resident buying offices are set up as extension services to stores and, as experienced advisers, can bring a knowledge of the field to the novice. A steady reading of the trade papers will familiarize you with names of resident buying offices, as will the yellow pages of major market cities such as New York, Chicago, Miami, Dallas, Los Angeles and St. Louis.

Merchandise brokers offer a whole different service. They also "represent" the shop owners in the market but are paid commissions by the manufacturers whose goods they sell to the shop owners. Stores subscribing to a broker service pay no fee but are responsible for covering the cost of phone calls and wires from the broker. There is a contract signed by both parties. Most brokers also send member stores a series of market-coverage bulletins, pushing new items and fast-reorder items.

In order to interest a broker, a shop has to go through a vigorous credit check, which usually eliminates the newcomer who has no credit. Also, brokers can only work well with stores of sizable volume or with several branches, guaranteeing a steady turnover of trendy merchandise.

Many shop owners swear by their buying offices or brokers, saying they couldn't be in business without them. Many others never have anything to do with these services, preferring to utilize their own resources. And some stores begin by belonging to a buying office and later drop the service when they have built up their own knowledge of the market and are familiar with dealing with suppliers.

Another method of bringing merchandise into a small shop is through consignment. Unique fashions and home furnishings accessories and crafts are often handled this way, as are very large and/or very costly pieces. Consignment is a loan arrangement whereby the supplier lends items to the shopkeeper. If the work is sold, the shop owner gets a commission, usually one-third of the selling price. If the piece is not sold within the agreed-upon time, it is returned, hopefully in mint condition, to its rightful owner and the deal is off.

Consignment is looked on with joy by many retailers, as it keeps their shelves filled with interesting new stock at no cost to them. Consignment is also welcomed by designers of quick-selling works, since they generally get two-thirds of the selling price rather than the one-half they would get if the retailer bought the piece wholesale and then marked it up to retail. Consignment is often a way for the shop owner to test the salability of items made by new craftspeople. If the designs move quickly the shop owner usually will switch from consignment to straight wholesale purchasing.

Consignment, all in all, is not such a terrific deal for the craftsperson who does not have an avid following. Too often the consignment merchandise is returned in poor condition, after long delays. Other craftspeople complain that consignment items are offered last to customers, only after the customer has made it clear she is not interested in the regular stock—the stock the shop owner's own money is tied up in. Be ready to deal with these complaints when you discuss consignment with designers. By organizing your consignment business adequately, you can wipe out many of the objections and make it work for both you and the consignee.

The Small Business Administration outlines such organization in their booklet *Starting and Managing a Swap Shop or a Consignment Sale Shop*, by Henry A. Ware. According to Mr. Ware, a lot depends on a clear understanding of the whole procedure between the shop owner and the designer. He recommends the following set of rules for consignment and suggests they be printed on the back of the consignment receipt, to be read over, initialed and dated before any work is placed in the shop:

1. Articles may be brought in for consignment at any time during shop hours.
2. Only articles in perfect condition will be accepted.
3. The shop's decision on acceptance is final.
4. Checks covering all items sold for consignors during a calendar month will be mailed during the first week of the following month.
5. Articles not sold within a month after the first of the month following consignment will be reduced in price at the discretion of the management.
6. Articles not sold within 3 months after the first month following consignment will be removed from inventory and should be picked up by the consignor.
7. The shop reserves the right to dispose of all articles unsold and unclaimed 4 months after the first of the month following consignment, without further notice to consignors and without liability on the part of the shop to consignors.
8. All reasonable care will be taken of articles consigned to the shop, but they are left at the owner's risk. The shop carries fire and vandalism insurance but assumes no responsibility

beyond reasonable care for theft or shop damage to articles.

9. The shop's commission on items sold is one-third of the actual selling price. There is no charge on items that do not sell.

An exception may be made to Rule 5, automatically reducing the prices of unsold pieces after the first month. If no price reductions are to be made, Rule 5 should be crossed out of the agreement at the time of signing.

The bookkeeping for consignment merchandise is different from your regular bookkeeping and should be kept separate. Mr. Ware suggests giving each consignee a number in sequence, preceded by the person's initials— e.g., designer Josephine Smith might become code number "S-10," indicating that she is the tenth person with a last name beginning with "S" who has pieces currently on consignment in the shop. This number/letter combination is then used on all records, receipts and tags.

The consignment receipt, with a carbon copy, is filled out when items are accepted for the shop. Initials are used to indicate departures from the regular rules. For example, NMD means "no markdown" and XX might indicate a partial markdown, but the price is not to drop below a certain pre-arranged figure.

As work is sold by the shop, the receipt is filled in, until the entire amount of merchandise is accounted for. A completed receipt might look like this:

3/15/77

THE WINDOWS SHOP
500 Main Street
Anytown, U.S.A. 00000
Phone: 000-123-4567

Consignor:

Josephine Smith
3 Pine Drive
Anytown, U.S.A. 00000
No. S-10

Item #	Description	Asking Price	Selling Price	Date Sold	Date Paid
1	Soup Tureen, Ladle	$50.00	$40.00	5/5	6/3
1	Salad Bowl NMD	37.00	37.00	3/25	4/10
3	Wall Mirror XX	43.00	40.00	6/12	7/5

Open Tuesday through Saturday 10–6 except Friday 10–9
See shop rules for consignment on reverse side

. The price tags on consignment merchandise must follow the code used on the receipt. In the case of Josephine Smith's items, the tags would look like theseG

S-10	S-10	S-10
# 1	# 2	# 3
Soup Tureen & Ladle	Salad Bowl NMD	Wall Mirror XX
$50.00	$37.00	$43.00

The final step in consignment—record keeping—is the daily sales tally, translating all the transactions and abbreviations into dollars and cents. Keep the consignment tallies in a separate book so they don't become confused with your other daily records.

At the end of each day sort out the sales slips that have the letter/number code on them, indicating a consignment sale. Enter the necessary information for that day into the consignment book and fill in the blanks on your copy of the consignment receipt. Then, when check-paying time rolls around, go through the consignment tally book, issue payments and enter the date paid on your copy of the consignment receipts.

A filled-in page of your daily consignment sales book might look like this (if you have sales tax, add a column for it and do a total so you'll know each day what amount you have to send along to the government):

DAILY CONSIGNMENT SALES BOOK

October 28, 1977

Consignor's #	Date	Item #	Description	Selling Price	Commission
A-11	8/6	4	Lace apron	$12.00	$4.00
D-7	8/9	1	Vase	$30.00	10.00
C-9	9/11	8	Place mat set	15.00	5.00
J-2	10/15	6	Tray	75.00	25.00

TOTAL SALES AND COMMISSIONS $132.00 $44.00

MINUS COMMISSIONS −44.00

TOTAL DUE CONSIGNORS $88.00

Another way of getting merchandise into your shop is to manufacture it yourself, becoming both wholesaler and retailer. This has advantages and disadvantages. On the plus side, it allows you to create a specialty shop independent of what is out on the commercial market. Nobody can truly compete with you because nobody can offer the same stock. It also allows you the opportunity to concentrate on your own best sellers and wholesale them to other shops in other parts of the country.

The negatives can be summed up succinctly: it's an unbelievable amount of work! People do it and they make lots of money at it, enough usually to hire a person to be in charge of whatever part of the operation they least enjoy. In order for the system to work, the wholesaling and retailing operations must be kept scrupulously separate.

If you decide to go this route, you must select a way of costing your products so you can make money on them if you wholesale and also if you retail them yourself. There are many costing formulas for duplicative* items, but all of them deal with four crucial elements: direct materials cost, direct labor cost, overhead expenses and profit.

The success of your costing formula depends on how well these four elements relate to each other. If you leave any one of them out of the formula, you're really up a tree. Everything you design to be sold must be costed separately, and any change in design or manufacture necessitates a revision in the original costing. When you first start to cost, it seems to take forever, but the more you do the speedier it gets, until you find yourself designing with the costing formula in mind.

Begin by taking one item and listing on paper all the materials that go into making it. Have the item in front of you so you can check off every tiny part, every whiff of lacquer spray, every button. Then figure out as nearly as you can what each component cost—dividing into parts of a dozen, fractions of a pound—and list the approximate amounts of money next to the item. Add these up and you know pretty accurately what the direct materials cost is.

Next figure out the amount of labor that goes into mak-

---

*This is a standard word among craftspeople meaning a design that has been created specifically to be copied or reproduced a number of times unlike something made up as a "one-of-a-kind" piece.

ing the item—not the work put into designing it, but the work hours necessary to duplicate it once the design is established. Try to think of it in terms of modest mass production, having several items in the works at one time. Once you've arrived at a certain number of hours/minutes needed, check it out again and be sure you've included adequate preparation and clean-up time.

Then shop around and see what you would have to pay somebody else to do the production work. You may not choose to pay anybody else, but if you get into production wholesaling, you'll need to hire help, so build adequate amounts of pay into your initial costing. This part often requires outside research. Be accurate with the labor costs: it's one place mistakes can be fatal and you can end up losing money on every item you produce. Finally, write down the amount of money it will cost you to have one item duplicated. That's your direct labor cost.

The third part of the formula is your overhead. This is not going to be totally accurate either, but be as accurate as you can. Overhead covers everything necessary to maintain the place within which you produce your items: rent, electricity, telephone, machinery or equipment, stationery, wrapping paper, insurance, repairs and maintenance, etc.

Do the best you can, figuring out what part of your total space you use for manufacturing and what part for retailing. Divide up the light and phone bills, the insurance and so on. It's important that you build into your wholesale price a bit of money to contribute toward each of these expenses. The combination of what you make from wholesaling and what you make from retailing is what will or will not pay your bills. Total up your overhead for one month. Then divide into the figure the number of pieces you can produce during one month, so each thing you make can carry a tiny bit of your total monthly expenses.

If you're producing many different styles, divide the total monthly production figure into your overhead, spreading the amount of money you need to raise to cover your wholesaling over the entire group of things you plan to make. No piece should be sold that does not bring back a little money to put toward paying the overhead.

The fourth element in any costing formula is the profit—how much money you want to make on each item you sell after all the expenses of producing it are covered. The profit figure also entails some outside research so that you can get an idea of what similar pieces are priced at. Add to your research your own idea of how much you could retail the work for, using the regular markup you would use on merchandise bought from an outside supplier. This is generally double the wholesale price— e.g., an item bought wholesale for $25 would be marked up to $50 retail.

For example, you might find you can produce a handbag for $15—this being the total of your direct materials cost, direct labor cost and overhead expenses for that one item. You check other stores and decide what you could get for it in your own shop. Say it looks as if it could be priced at $40 retail. This indicates a $20 wholesale price, which would bring you a profit figure of $5 per bag sold wholesale.

Sometimes the costing formula works out to show you that you can't produce a piece to sell at what you feel is the right price. Then the design must be re-evaluated and revised, the list of materials reconsidered for less expensive substitutions and the overhead checked out with an eye to cutting costs. There are enough places to modify costs that most designs for production can be shaped into money makers. It's a question of refiguring and refiguring.

A variation on wholesaling is to produce your own merchandise without ever wholesaling to other shops. The four basic costing elements (labor, materials, overhead, profit) still must be taken into consideration. Sometimes these are lumped together into two divisions—one-half of the retail price covers the cost of making the item, and the other half covers the cost of selling it, and includes the profit. In other words, labor and materials would be the first half and overhead and profit would complete the formula. In this way you would see how much money you are really making and how much profit various different items bring in.

Whichever costing formula you choose to use, you still should do research in competitive stores and catalogues. Prices are made in the marketplace. The deciding factor in setting your prices is always how and where each item fits into the overall supply and demand for your area.

9

Display

"If the store doesn't project an image within which the customer will spend $50, then the customer will adjust to the image the store projects—and spend less." This is the way New York design consultant Barnett Simons, president of Instant Interiors Inc., describes the importance of display. Pre-conditioning is the key word, and it applies to all interior furnishings and lighting within your shop.

The Simons theory is easily tested. Set foot in Tiffany's and you know by subtle inference that you will spend Money. Stroll into Woolworth's and you know you'll spend a lot less. The messages you get from the decor are carefully planned out; nothing happens by accident.

Define your message before you look at a single fixture. Think through what you feel will indicate the levels of quality and price in your shop. Discount shops and outlet centers can afford to have wares displayed on wire racks and in cardboard bins. A more expensive boutique can display the same amount of merchandise on contoured hangers or arranged in elegant wicker baskets. Select your look and plan toward achieving it.

Traffic flow is the first consideration because it tells you how much of what you can put where. The ideal shop interior plan takes the customer as she enters the store and leads her subtly past most of the merchandise on her way back out onto the street. This is done by furnishing, light and color. The more she can see, the more she has to consider buying. The ultimate aim of all display is to convert the shopper into a buyer.

(Traffic flow is also important as a safeguard against shoplifting. The floor plan must be open enough to allow complete visibility of all selling space at all times and to allow the staff to move easily and quickly into the different selling areas. Small, easily pocketable items should never be placed on open display units near an exit.)

Certain areas in every shop are considered "hot" by retailers:

- The first major selling area the customer sees when she walks in the door—wherever her eye falls first.
- Near the cash register: customers always have to wait for purchases to be written up and wrapped, so give them plenty of impulse items to look at while they wait.
- Near try-on rooms: again, a waiting spot, a natural for an accessories display.
- Next to any sort of community bulletin board or message center.

Other considerations for a small store are:

- Placement of the cash box: In a one-person operation the money will be left untended some of the time, so the register or box should be placed in the spot least accessible to the public. Never place the cash box near a door or open on a table.

- Fire laws: Check requirements with your local fire station before you get too far into planning. Some localities require aisles of certain measurements, a specific number of exits in ratio to the square footage of the shop, etc.

If you have the extra money, a great way to get this all together is to hire a consulting architect or interior designer and work with him or her to design an attractive and efficient floor plan. Fees for consultations vary in different parts of the country, generally beginning around $75 for an advisory session and suggested floor plan. If you intend to use a consultant, check some installations she has done and verify how pleased the employers were with the practicality of his or her designs—as you would with any outside supplier. Before your consultation understand exactly what the fee is buying you in terms of time and on-paper planning.

A consultant will be able to do much more for you if you have sorted out your thoughts before the consultation. Bring precise ideas of your likes and dislikes to the meeting. Be able to tell what feeling you want customers to have when they come to your shop. Show magazine or newspaper clippings of shops that you find especially attractive. The clearer you are, the more time you can save, and the better the results will be.

As with most professions, there is no way to duplicate expertise with enthusiastic do-it-yourself efforts. However, you can use some designer methods to make sense out of your space if you don't plan to hire a consultant. Step one is the drawing up of an accurate floor plan.

Get some graph paper from the stationers', and obtain a long tape measure or carpenter's folding rule. Establish a ratio of squares to measured feet—say, one square equals one foot—and begin measuring your shop space. Indicate all windows, doors, closets or built-in cupboards, the direction the doors open and pipes and heating units. Transfer the measurements to the graph paper, creating a small-scale drawing of your entire area.

Once you've got the drawing reasonably accurate, study the possibilities for aisle locations. Obviously the main entrance is the beginning of the first aisle, bringing the customer into the shop and starting her on the route around the establishment. Many shops set up a low showcase or table in the center of the room, creating a circular path around the room. This effectively brings the customer into eye contact with merchandise on both sides of the store. Avoid "figure eight" aisles; the back loop ends up with a lot less traffic than the front.

Aisle widths less than 4½ feet will prove difficult during crowded selling hours, but spaciousness is sometimes sacrificed in order to display the optimum amount of merchandise. Traffic can be guided by judicious placement of display units, by floor-covering materials, by lighting and by color. However, for purposes of creating a scale floor plan, cut graph-paper strips to scale to indicate aisles and play around with placing them in different spots on your plan.

Treat display tables, shelving, clothing racks, cabinets, etc. the same way—cut shapes out of graph paper to scale and move them around on the floor plan to explore the advantages of different arrangements. Be relatively accurate in cutting out scale-model shapes for the furnishings so when the time comes to build, borrow or buy the actual units, you will have your measurements in hand. You increase your decorating possibilities if you avoid large built-in units and if you use easily paintable building materials. Periodic furniture rearranging and repainting will give you fresh, new-looking interiors at minimal cost.

The use of antique furniture as display pieces often adds

charm and warmth to a shop interior. Check your insurance company for a policy rider that covers damage while in transit and on display—a pursuasive argument when dealing with collectors.

There are two standard arrangements for procuring antiques for display:

Rental	The fee is approximately 25 percent of the purchase price for one month's use. Full insurance coverage is usual, and the shop owner arranges pick-up and delivery of the items or is billed by the dealer for the service.
Borrowing	No fee is charged, but the purchase price of the piece plus the dealer's name and address are prominently displayed. Full insurance coverage is usual, and the pick-up and delivery is negotiable, as is a commission fee in case the shop owner sells the piece.

Whether or not you choose antiques, keep nondisplay unit furnishings to a minimum. Include a ladder or two—a great way to utilize vertical display space. Ladders work equally well in the front window or on low platforms anywhere in the shop. Merchandise can be draped over rungs, signs can be propped on them. Ladders can be easily painted, are portable and fold compactly for storage.

Plants are currently in vogue as the decorative accessory to bring freshness and life into a room. This may be true for residential interiors, but be wary of tucking plants all over your shop unless you plan to sell them.

Plants require stabilized conditions and a lot of care in order to look fabulous. They also shift focus away from your stock.

After you have worked out some acceptable floor-plan placements, begin dealing with the ceiling, walls and floor. Ceilings are important only to hang things from. The ceiling should not intrude into the customer's awareness and dilute the impact of the displayed merchandise. If the ceiling is in good shape and is reasonably good-looking, paint it a light color. If it's terrible, paint it dark and it will lose itself and cease being a distraction.

Floors should not be attention-grabbers either, so use neutral tones. Traffic flow can be controlled somewhat by using two different materials to mark out the path you want the customer to take around the shop. Combinations of tile and carpeting are effective; the shoppers will tend to follow the tile "road" as it curves around the display units. Similarly, contrasting colors of paint can be used to mark a path for the customer. Coat all painted floors with polyurethane to make them practical and long-wearing. Keep floors spotless; make vacuuming and mopping part of your daily routine.

The walls in a small shop will form the background for most of your vertical displays, so select two contrasting materials for variation. Some merchandise will look best against a dark background; others against a light one. Wood paneling is often used for the darker area, as it is relatively inexpensive, can be installed by a nonprofessional and requires little upkeep.

Cover bad walls with posters or maps glued with wallpaper paste. Old newspapers, magazine covers, sheet music and book jackets are other low-budget wall brighteners that can add charm. Don't shellac over the papers so you can glue fresh ones right over the old ones whenever you want. If possible use items that are appropriate to the merchandise you are selling. For example, an African shop could have a large, attractive map of Africa as part of the decor.

Sometimes walls are in such bad shape that covering them with paper is impossible. A scenic design trick works well to camouflage disasters and still give a flexibility to your interior. Measure the damaged walls and get two wooden battens—small strips of lumber—cut to the width of the walls you wish to cover. Buy enough lightweight, opaque fabric to cover the walls nearly double the width measurement, cut it into strips the height of the wall and staple it top and bottom onto the battens, gathering it as you staple. Try for an even fullness, leaving enough sticking up at the top and bottom to cover the battens. Then screw or nail the battens into the top and bottom of the wall—or even to the ceiling and floor if necessary. Take it all down to launder periodically. Staple new fabric up to redecorate.

Color, always a controversial topic in decorating, becomes even more of a problem for retailers. Some hold that the ideal background color is a neutral pastel shade, others say bright primary colors make a place look exciting, still another group opts for feminine colors on the theory that most retail customers are women. Whatever your preference, you would do well to stick with one family of color—for example, using beige, cream and ivory with brown. As long as your selections are all generically related, you won't go too far wrong. Mix warm colors with cool colors and you might run into trouble.

Shop the decorating magazines for color schemes you find pleasing, with an eye to how your merchandise will look against it. No matter what advice you get from others, make the place as pleasant for yourself as you can. You are the person who will be spending the most time there.

After you have gotten the structure of your shop out of the way, concentrate on lighting. If customers can't see the merchandise, they won't buy it. And even if they can see it, if it looks washed-out and unattractive they still won't buy it. Lighting is all-important to any shop, large or small.

As with space planning, if you have the extra money, hire a qualified lighting designer to create a system of illumination that will show your shop to best advantage. Do some research in advance of your consultation so you can tell the designer what you find pleasing, and show her some clippings if you can.

If you don't have the extra money you can do it yourself, using some of the professional lighting methods to build in style and flexibility. First, a quick review of light from your first-year physics class:

- In 1666 Sir Isaac Newton passed a beam of light through a prism and discovered that it contained all the colors of the rainbow.

- Light that looks white is generally shaded either to warm (red/yellow) or cool (blue/purple) and therefore will distort the colors of merchandise displayed in it.

The most workable lighting plan for a small shop consists of general, flat, overall illumination so the customers can see their way around, plus carefully placed spotlights that focus attention on certain display areas and highlight the stock. Since you will want to keep the shop looking new and different by periodically changing the display areas, the spotlights should be somewhat portable. The general illumination is stationary, and therefore can be built-in.

Without getting into exotic lighting equipment you have

your choice of incandescent or fluorescent light. The optimum lighting plan will use both, combining them for color accuracy, contrast, energy-saving and economy factors.

Incandescents give a warm light and are easily directed to highlight specific areas. They are less efficient than fluorescent, generate more heat and have a shorter life.

Fluorescents provide good economy, efficiency and long life. They give a rather flat, general light and generate little heat.

There are a number of incandescent and fluorescent lamps:

Incandescents: available in wattages from 15 to 1500 in many sizes, shapes and colors.

General service: the standard bulbs used in home fixtures.

Reflector lamps: photofloods and photospots, made with a built-in reflector that bounces the light through the front surface of the lamp. The floods reflect light in a general area, with some spillover. The spots focus the light into a more condensed area and have more clearly defined edges.

Tungsten-hologen lamp: a small but powerful spotlight.

Fluorescents: Available in a wide range of shades including:

        Cool White
        DeLuxe Cool White
        Standard Warm White
        DeLuxe Warm White
        White
        Daylight

Use the following chart to compare the color-rendition effects of incandescents and fluorescents:

Type	Tint Given White Surface	Blue	Green	Red
Incandescent	Light orange	Dulls, darkens	Darkens, brown hues	Enhances
Tungsten-halogen	Light yellow	Dulls, darkens, yellowish hue	Deep shades warmed, darkens, yellows	Enhances, slight yellowing
Cool white fluorescent	Slight blue	Grays, darkens	Grays, except blues and greens	Grays and darkens
DeLuxe cool white fluorescent	None	Lighter, clearer, cooler	Clear, light	Clear, rich, vibrant
Standard warm white fluorescent	Light yellow	Clear, rich	Light shades bright, clear	Light shades bright and clear
DeLuxe warm white fluorescent	Slight yellow	Warms, deepens	Enriches, warms, deepens	Bright, rich
White fluorescent	Slight yellow	Grays darker shades, clears light shades	Bright, slight yellowing	Dulls dark shades, yellows light shades
Daylight Fluorescent	Light blue	Cools, enhances	Brightens, blues	Grays, dulls, gives violet hue

The energy crisis will be with us for the foreseeable future, so the energy comparison between fluorescent and incandescent lighting must be considered, as well as the economic comparison. The Illuminating Engineering Society furnishes the following data:

	Incandescent Bulb	DeLuxe Fluorescent Tube	Advantages of Fluorescent
Watts	75	30 (44 total input watts)	31-watt (or 41%) energy saving
Rates life	750 hours	15,000 hours	lasts 14,250 hours more, or 20 times longer
Amount of light	1180 lumens	1530 lumens	350 more lumens, or 30% more light

The Society also furnishes data comparing the lumen output (amount of light) between the standard incandescent and the long-life incandescent bulbs, showing that the standard bulb puts out a lot more light than the comparable long-life bulb. They suggest checking the lumen ratings printed on the light bulb package: the higher the lumens, the more light you are buying.

What all these data point to for the lighting plan you are working on is that fluorescents are a better buy all around, but will only give you flat general lighting. Incandescents are more expensive and less efficient but are the logical supplements to highlight the merchandise.

Refer to your floor plan and note display areas that call for intense brightness—usually around the walls, the front windows and a center island, if you have one. Also mark out the section, generally over the aisles, that can have less illumination, setting up a contrast that will make the shop look more interesting.

If your budget is low, the incandescent fixtures can be simple clip-on photographer's reflector lights used with a standard light bulb. Slightly more money will buy you swivel bases to use with reflector spotlights and floodlights. Since the reflectors are built in on these, no additional metal reflector is needed.

A more costly setup is the track lighting found in galleries, now sold for general use. Here you purchase a length of metal track that is fastened to the ceiling. Small spotlights are hung from the track and can be moved around on it and swiveled on a universal socket to focus light wherever it is needed. Track lengths and spotlights are generally sold separately and are ideal for more permanent installations.

Simple fluorescent tubes suspended from the ceiling are fine for general lighting. If you want to control the spill of light, buy fixtures with louver units that channel the light downward—inexpensive but effective.

Plan incandescent lights focused to wash the upper walls of the shop, creating supplemental display areas above shelves and merchandise racks. The more display areas you can create, the more you can tempt the customers into buying. A display rule for shops selling apparel is to accessorize as many displays as possible. Show a sweater along with scarf, jewelry, belt, cap, gloves, etc. Display a child's jumper over a turtleneck, and pin coordinating tights to hang down underneath. Sell a total look.

Always display your best sellers. It might seem redundant to set out the items that go flying out of the store on their own, but by displaying the "hotsies" you reinforce the image of your shop as a leader. You have exactly what people are looking for exactly when they are looking.

Keep the nonsellers discreetly de-emphasized so you don't parade mistakes in front of the public.

Some shops plan a sale corner or a markdown table in their initial floor plan. It is usually placed toward the interior of the shop, since it can be used to bring customers into different parts of the shop, showing them nonsale merchandise they might otherwise not notice.

The balance of light intensities between your various lighting units should vary with the displays. Keep the fluorescents all the same but vary the wattage on the spotlights so that some displays will sparkle a bit more than others. Some lighting textbooks suggest that special super-sale displays should be as much as 2½ times brighter than the regular displays.

Studies have been establishing the recommended illumination levels for various parts of a shop. The Illuminating Engineering Society's *Lighting Handbook* suggests the following:

Recommended Illumination Levels
for Stores

Interior	Foot-candles
Circulation areas	30
Merchandise areas	100–200
Showcases and wall cases	200–500
Feature displays	500
Dressing areas	50
Fitting areas	200
Stock rooms	30
Rest rooms	30
General lighting on vertical surfaces	200
Feature displays	1000

Exterior

Building floodlighting	
(depending on light or dark surfaces)	
Bright surroundings	15–50
Dark surroundings	5–20
Parking areas	1–2

Foot-candles are measurements we don't normally deal with. Lighting engineers use specialized equipment to meter foot-candles, but for your planning purpose, a pretty accurate measurement of foot-candles can be made using the exposure meter on a camera. Here are two methods:

Method 1:   Set the film-speed dial to ASA 100 and aim the camera or hand-held meter at a sheet of matte white cardboard or paper in the proposed location and orient it to the maximum light source. Get close enough to the paper so the meter sees only the white paper. Be sure not to block the light or create a shadow. The shutter speed indicated opposite stop f4, read as a whole number, will be the approximate foot-candles of illumination measured. For example, if the f-stop (lens opening) registers an exposure of 1/250 second, there are about 250 foot-candles of light playing on the white sheet.

Method 2:   Set the ASA film speed at 200

and the shutter speed at 1/125 second. Focus on the white paper as above. Adjust the f-stop until a correct exposure is shown in the light meter in the camera. Use the table below to find out how many foot-candles you have:

f2.8	32 foot-candles
f4	64
f5.6	125
f8	250
f11	500
f16	1000
f22	2000

Take care when placing the spotlights around that they are always enough in front of the merchandise to light the entire area without casting great shadows. If shadows become a problem, use two smaller spots focused at 45-degree angles, hitting the merchandise from each side. Place overhead spotlights slightly in front of display cases having glass tops to avoid glaring reflections. If your decor permits, place a row of footlights in the front window for an "on stage" effect.

Change displays to keep pace with store traffic. For example, shops in a resort area should change displays each Thursday during the tourist season to attract weekend vacationers. Get to know the pay schedules of your regular customers: if people get their paychecks twice a month, change your displays a day or two before every payday, and pick up extra "money-in-the-pocket" sales.

Keep a display calendar in tune with national and local holidays and special events. Even Groundhog Day can be the theme of a window display, with plump brown-paper-bag groundhogs peeking around the merchandise. Manufacturers and distributors often supply gratis seasonal promotion material, so be sure to check your resources for Christmas, Easter, etc. Unfortunately a lot of the "freebie" display aids look a bit too mass-produced to be used in a super-special shop or boutique, but sometimes portions of them are applicable.

Aside from the Christmas season, which seems to get longer every year, a special holiday display will sell goods for two weeks in advance. For periods longer than two weeks plan two separate displays, each a version of the holiday theme. As soon as the holiday is past, change the displays immediately. Stash the bunnies away on Easter Monday. Quick changes in your window displays are also a good safeguard against damage to stock from dirt and sun fading.

Keep display areas spotless. New merchandise will look instantly dreary if placed on dusty props surrounded with tired tissue, leaves, etc. Backgrounds are especially vulnerable. If you have any doubt about the usability of a background, scrap it and put in something fresh. The first impression sets the stage for sales.

There are two schools of thought on the use of signs. Some retailers feel that signs are a sales plus, worth the expense, helping to answer obvious customer questions. Others avoid signs, saying that without them the customer is brought into contact with the sales person, who will then be able to suggest alternatives and additions. Whichever route you take, some signs are inevitable, and they must be clear, clean and large enough to be easily read.

10

Advertising

Advertising is often viewed as the magic ingredient that can make or break a business. It's easy to forget that while advertising will help put your shop on the map, it will not guarantee you a successful, profitable venture.

Begin with the assumption that you do not *have* to advertise. Many shops do well on publicity. On the other hand, successful advertising will keep your name in front of the public, remind people of what you are selling and fan their desire to come into your shop and buy.

If you have the money, it's a good way to spend it. However, advertising is only as good as the product. The shop has to be easily accessible, adequately staffed, well stocked and open for business before advertising can do any good. Check your priorities before setting up an advertising budget.

Advertising is only as good as it is repetitive. If you can't see your way clear to run a minimum of four ads per year, you would be better off putting your money into other forms of promotion. Human beings are forgetful types. An ad reminding them of you every three months is about as long as you can go without being forgotten.

There is no rigid rule about the amount of money that should be spent on advertising. You might decide to allocate 2 percent of your estimated yearly gross sales—a common advertising budget amount—or you might opt for 10 percent. Or you might just sit it out for the first year except for "Compliments Of " ads in school and charity yearbooks and the Chamber of Commerce magazine.

There are several categories of advertising for you to consider:

- Newspapers
    Display advertisements
    Personal-column ads
- Magazines
    Display advertisements
    Shopping-column ads
- Radio and Television
    Spot announcements

Magazines and weekly newspapers have the advantage of being kept around longer than the daily paper, so your ad might be seen several different times, and/or passed along to a large number of extra readers. Radio spot announcements have the advantage of urgency, great to highlight a one-day happening, but normally too expensive to be plausible for a new, small shop. And television, with impressive production costs, is out of reach for most medium-sized businesses.

Evaluate what is available to you in your area by reading and listening to everything that is offered. Consult your customer profile to determine what your customers might be reading or listening to.

For newspapers and magazines, go to your local library and check back issues to see which ads have been repeated and repeated over the past 6 to 12 months. You can assume that these companies were getting enough of a response from their ads that they were satisfied to keep running more. Notice if and how the copy changes in the long-running ads. You will find certain sizes and kinds of ads turning up regularly in each publication; couple this information with the repetitiveness count and you will usually come up with the kind and type of ad that does best in that medium.

Then write or call the advertising department of the paper or magazine and request circulation information, which will tell you how many readers they believe they have, who they are and where they come from. Readers are not necessarily subscribers or newsstand purchasers, so ask how they have arrived at their totals to get some idea of what the publication feels is the pass-along life of each issue. Also ask the advertising department to give you facts on what the most popular size of display ad is, and what is the frequency of insertion most often scheduled.

See how all this tallies up with your own assumptions from your library research, and how their readership profile compares with your own customer profile. If you feel that there is a vast difference between what you observed and what the publication is claiming, do not hesitate to ask for an explanation. It's your money you are spending, no matter how little of it, and you owe it to yourself to spend it wisely.

Betty Allen, president of M. E. Allen Associates, Marketing Services, and a former vice-president of Ted Bates & Co., fifth largest advertising agency in the world, stresses that point when working with small-business people. "Don't be humble. Remember, you're the customer when dealing with the media. And if you're uncomfortable with your advertising, question it. Get the best buy for your money."

Note the location of the readers as described by the circulation data. Look to broaden your base of sales, extending your message outside the local area. Advertising that merely resells to your regular customers will do a lot less for you than advertising that brings you new acquaintances.

Ask for rates. All publications have frequency discounts—the more you run, the cheaper it gets. But don't let a cheap offer con you. You know your budget, and your own buying habits. Several retailers interviewed said they make it a rule to wait a full week between getting advertising information and signing a space contract. This gives them time to regain their perspective after being swept away by the advertising salesman's "buy-now" presentation.

Before you sign, make sure you understand all parts of the space contract, especially the termination clauses. Find out what it will really cost you if you find you want to get out from under a yearly advertising campaign. And know how your money will be credited if you are doing so fabulously that you want to increase either space or frequency, canceling the existing contract and taking out a larger one.

Sound out the advertising department about any "specials" that go along with advertising space. Occasionally directories or group listings are published by the same companies. And, of course, access to the editorial staff is important, even though most publications will claim that their advertising and editorial people have absolutely no contact. Let the claims go unchallenged, but do suggest that pick-up of your publicity releases would be appreciated and helpful since advertising and publicity have similar aims. . . .

Once you've decided to advertise, you have your choice of doing "institutional" or "product" advertising. Institutional ads merely remind the reader that your shop exists, at your address, with your phone, and is open during your hours. The institutional ad might include a phrase, repeated in every ad, that identifies the type of business you are in:

"The Potter's Outlet"

"Clothes for Kids from Birth to Teens"

"Specialists in Early American Antiques"

The product ad, in contrast, tells the reader about a specific piece of merchandise. Product ads have more of a sense of urgency to them, prodding the reader to move quickly to take advantage of the advertised offer. The specialness of the offer should be justified:

"Overstock on Handthrown Mugs—25% Off—One Week Only"

"Just Arrived—Appalachian Patchwork Smocks"

"Our Buying Trip Was A Success—
Stop In and See the New Treasures!"

It is difficult to say whether institutional or product advertising should be chosen. Very tiny ads sometimes seem to prohibit the product approach, but with skillful design you can bring out many successful small product ads. A good guide is to consider how many ads you plan on running and to see how that relates to special product offers (*not* just price cuts) that you can see yourself coming up with.

When the time comes for you to design your first set of ads, ask for help from the media department of the publication that will be running them. Most newspapers and magazines have somebody on their staff who works with small advertisers, showing them what sort of thing they can do in the space they have purchased.

Since repetition is what you are after, selecting one format and sticking to it for all your ads makes the most sense. If you decide to supplement your advertising with handbills, try to repeat the look of your ads in the fliers. Anything you can do to implant your image in the minds of the public will pay off.

If you come up with a dynamite logo—a visual presentation of your shop's name—be sure to use it on everything you have printed, from shopping bags to sales checks. Or have a rubber stamp made of your distinctive logo so you can individualize everything while you are getting the money together for a professional printing job.

If the media department of your chosen publication is not able to advise you, get some tracing paper and set out on your own ad-designing session. First trace the size space you have contracted for so you know what you have to work with. Make a lot of blanks the size of your ad space.

Then make a list of the component parts of your ad—everything you want the reader to know:

1 Your shop's name
2 The complete, correct address
3 The complete telephone number
4 Hours the shop is open
5 What you are advertising (product)
6 Why you are advertising (justification)
7 Price of what you are advertising

The first job an advertisement has to do is to get the attention of the reader. This can be done a number of ways. Most common are the use of a startling headline or a unique placement of the elements of the ad, making it look visually different and more exciting than other ads the same size and shape. Look through newspapers, pick out ads you think are good and analyze them to see what caught your interest. You are not going to plagiarize, you are just looking for background knowledge.

Begin sketching ideas on some of the blanks you have traced. Just draw in lines where you want the lettering to fit, and use rough shapes to show the logo, etc. Make six or eight different sketches—the more the better.

Depending on the size of your space, you might want to do a replica of the merchandise. Photographs don't always reproduce well in newspapers, especially reduced in size. Consult a professional photographer before you get involved with planning ads illustrated with photographs. It runs into extra money and is often less effective than using all type or simple line drawing.

Simple is the key word in simple line drawing. No shading, little dimension, almost a cartoon of the item you are featuring will bring you better results than a more detailed sketch. Again, let the size of your ad dictate whether or not anything other than lettering and your logo should be included. White space surrounding type attracts much more attention than lines and letters crammed into every bit of space.

Depend on the advertising/media department of the publication to advise you on typefaces and the use of borders and other symbols. They will have certain stock items available for free to pretty up an ad. Also they will tell you whether or not a cut will have to be made of your logo for their printing process. A cut is a metal image of a design that is required in certain printing methods. If a cut is needed, you will be charged for it, but the price is nominal.

Once you arrive at a group of sketches that are acceptable to you, show them to others and get some reactions. Everybody who reads is an expert on advertising, so find out which of your ads will "pull" the most.

Large manufacturers who produce brand-name merchandise often have cooperative advertising arrangements available to the shops that buy from them. In some cases the manufacturer pays a large portion of the advertising space cost in return for a feature spot for his merchandise. Other brand-name suppliers offer a "mat service," wherein they supply an entire made-up, laid-out ad, ready for reproduction, with an empty space left for the shop to drop in their own name, address and logo.

Mat services are a mixed blessing. Little or no work is needed from you, the shop owner, in order to run the ad. However, the mat service ads will not look like the rest of your advertising and might be detrimental to the specific image you are building. This is especially true if you are seeking to be thought of as having wonderful items that can't be found elsewhere, shelves stocked with delights made especially for you. Still, cooperative advertising money makes too much sense as a budget extender to ignore, so check every large manufacturer's representative you deal with regularly.

Many small shops find that they are able to put together their own version of cooperative advertising. Location is generally the determinant; shops in one area will group their money and put out a series of ads inviting the public to enjoy the total shopping and entertainment possibilities of that area. Cooperative ads such as these can be converted into great giveaways in all the member stores by photocopying the ad and then printing something useful on the other side, such as a walking trail map or a calendar of upcoming events.

Magazine advertising operates rather like newspaper advertising. First, research the magazines to decide if they offer enough impact on your locality. An ad for a ski sweater will have little impact on a reader in Miami. Some magazines offer regional advertising space buys, allowing the advertiser to select East Coast, West Coast, Middle America and so forth. Regionals cost less and offer better concentration.

The type of magazine advertising that makes sense for the small shop is the shop-by-mail section found in the back of most consumer magazines. These are the small ads, usually with a sketch or photograph, offering the item via direct mail, prepaid, freight costs included. The shop-by-mail sections are expensive if compared with newspaper advertising rates but are less expensive than any other type of magazine advertising.

They are a great way to capitalize on any proven best-sellers you have in your shop. Many small retailers use direct mail to get extra milage out of every high-volume item. Setting up for this kind of direct-mail selling often involves nothing more than checking your post office for freight rates and lining up adequate shipping cartons that will be accepted by the local post office.

If you see a winner developing among your merchandise, an item not available from coast to coast, you would be smart to check out the consumer magazines shop-by-mail sections. Research to find similar kinds of merchandise, noticing the price and the ad presentation. Get back issues of the publication and see how many times the ads are repeated. Repetition, again, will signal to you the ads that are successful.

Narrow down which magazines seem right for your merchandise, and write to the advertising manager requesting circulation figures, reader profile and success stories of items similar to yours. You don't have to be too careful about giving out information on your top-secret, about-to-be-launched-nationally money maker. The advertising manager is there to sell you space, not to copy your idea.

Some consumer publications, notably the home-furnishings and decorating magazines, have a policy of swapping paid shop-by-mail ads for inclusion in the editorial "Best Buys of the Month" shopping column. Check over back issues and determine whether this policy might work for you. If most of the shopping-column items are also shown in adjacent small ads, you can be pretty sure there is an arrangement, so ask for details on that in your letter to the advertising manager.

Ads for the shop-by-mail section can be made up the same way as newspaper ads. Make a whole lot of blank ad shapes and draw up your list of what you must include, like complete mailing directions and a correct amount of money to cover postage and handling—i.e., total shipping costs.

Since all the shop-by-mail ads are product-oriented, you would be smart to hire a professional photographer to take clear, well-lighted photographs and furnish you with 8″ × 10″ glossy prints suitable for magazine reproduction. The success of the ad depends largely on how the merchandise looks, so don't try to do it yourself. The photographer will be helped if you show her copies of the magazine you are going to be in, so she can tailor her work to your needs.

Once you've invested in the photographs, you're set up to run duplicate advertisements in any number of competing publications. This is an alternative approach to running consecutive ads in one magazine and is more logical for shop-by-mail selling.

The importance of repetition and building up a consumer image that is so crucial in newspaper advertising diminishes for direct-mail ads. The shopping-column ad either sells or does not sell the reader on sight—she sees the picture of the product, wants it and orders it, or she turns the page and that's that. Who you are or what kind of shop you have makes little difference. Each product will succeed or fail on its own.

By running the identical ad in shop-by-mail sections of several magazines, you greatly extend your potential market and are able to trim costs down. By monitoring each publication's responses, you will build up a familiarity with the types of items that go best in the different magazines, so future advertising plans can be based on your own past experience.

Monitoring is done by including a "key" in the address in each ad you run. For example, one set of ads might read:

The Garden Shop   The Garden Shop
Dept. A   Dept. B
222 Main Street   222 Main Street
Your City, Your State 00000   Your City, Your State 00000

Each magazine is keyed to a different letter of the alphabet—e.g., Dept. A, Dept. B—or to the beginning letters of the publication's title. It's best done with letters rather than numbers, which sometimes get mixed up with the street address, the selling price and the postage-and-handling fee.

You'll be able to get a sound idea of what works best in which publication, so keep track of your responses and file them away for future comparisons. If you restrict your shop-by-mail efforts to only those items that have been your in-shop bestsellers, your chances of making some extra money are pretty good—provided your choice of magazine is appropriate.

Monitoring shop-by-mail advertising responses is not the only checking you have to do. It's important that you also keep track of results from the ads you run. Advertising is a means to an end; either it works for you or it doesn't.

Asking new customers how they happened to come into your shop is one way of testing the effectiveness of your ads. If you've put money into a series of ads, it stands to reason that somebody, somewhere, must be reading them. If nobody ever mentions noticing your ads, review them and consider taking a different approach for the next series.

There are many trade associations and councils that publish material about advertising developed to be helpful to the small retailer. An excellent list has been compiled by the Small Business Administration and is reprinted in the Appendix. Send out some postcards and ask for information.

Keep up with new trends in advertising. Begin noticing ads that especially appeal to you, even though they are not related to your field. Read trade newspapers for "success story" write-ups of other shops' advertising campaigns. The trade papers usually bring advance news of new methods and developments available to advertisers. When the scratch-and-smell chemical inks were introduced, features were run in the trade papers in virtually every field relating to retailing.

Experiment with anything that catches your fancy. The more imaginative your advertising, the more attention-getting it will be, and the more fun you will have planning and executing it. As long as you stay within your budget, how wrong can you go?

A funny story about do-it-yourself advertising is told by Mark Hanlon, owner, with his designer-wife, Wanda, of O Mistress Mine, a successful New York City boutique. Prior to joining up with Wanda's business, Mark had been working with some of the better New York advertising agencies. Mark still followed all the advertising trade papers and became interested in the development of subliminal advertising.

This was the period when much lip service was given to subliminal messages that could be blinked into regular television programming, creating in the viewer's subconscious an urge to buy. The viewers, not realizing what was hitting them, would not mount resistance to the subliminal commercials, so the advertising message would be more effective. Arguments were put forth on the ethics of subliminal advertising, likening it to brainwashing, manipulation of the public and no end of other evil doings.

Mark was fascinated. O Mistress Mine was not in a position to support any sort of television advertising campaign, but Mark was determined to test out subliminal power. After a quick survey of their resources he decided his subliminal campaign would have to be worked into the decor of the shop.

The main lighting fixture in the center of the ceiling had been replaced by 1920s mirrored ball that revolved, casting twinkly star-spots of light around the shop. The light reflections skittered across the ceiling rather rapidly and Mark felt the blinking effect was near enough to what he'd read about subliminal advertising to merit a try.

He lettered the word BUY on yards and yards of transparent tape, clipped it all into neat little squares and stuck the squares onto a random selection of surfaces of the mirrored ball. He spread the tapes around evenly so as not to reduce the sparkle. Then he turned the revolving motor on and sat back to monitor customer response.

As Wanda said later, Mark really took it all very well. Customers came and went. Business continued as usual, in keeping with last year's figures. His arms ceased aching from the hours spent on top of the ladder sticking the tape squares onto the mirrors. He had loads of information on the numbers and types of customers and what hours of the day they came into the shop—information they had always meant to gather.

And best of all, at cocktail parties Mark is able to say thoughtfully, "You know, that subliminal advertising everybody's been reading about? Well, it doesn't really work. . . ."

11

Publicity

When you hear people say, "Advertising costs a lot of money, but publicity is free," quickly remind yourself: (1) there's never a free lunch; (2) publicity isn't free—it's priceless. Priceless, because the best publicity you can ever hope to get happens when one of your satisfied customers tells somebody about your shop in such glowing terms that the listener can't wait to hurry over and check it out. It's the kind of occurrence you can't spend money to make happen, but it's the most efficient way to increase sales.

Publicity, public relations, consumer relations—whatever you want to call it—is the sum total of everything that creates a personality for your shop. Either it's good or it's mediocre, depending on how you design it. Some stores will be charming and sparkly, while others will be just another place to shop. Send your store to charm school if you have any doubts!

Begin with your store's visual appearance. The outside of your shop is the first thing the customer sees, so let it set the pace by creating excitement and anticipation. True, you are stuck with whatever the façade of the building looks like, but you can make sure your area is clean and freshly painted and your sign or banner is attractive and bright. The display windows are the "face" of your shop, so take care to keep them washed and well lighted.

Once the customer gets in the door, some reaction sets in—either positive or negative—to the layout of the place. Dust, stale air and general gloom are the most common negatives, and are also the easiest conditions to correct when they happen, or to design out before you open your doors. Daily cleanings, vacuumings and paint touch-ups are mandatory to maintain a "company's coming" look.

Some sort of sound system is a good idea, whether it be an expensive stereo or a modest AM radio. Sound should never become a distraction; use it to add to the overall pleasantness of the shop. Work toward having everything in the place contribute to good feelings.

Which brings us to the personnel who run the shop. No matter how wonderful the setting is, one grouch can put off every customer who strolls in. Make sure each new arrival is acknowledged with a smile, a nod, or words like, "Hi, are you looking for something specific or would you just like to look around a bit?" Your customers couldn't care less that you may be having the crisis of your adult life. They need to feel good about your shop or they'll soon go elsewhere to buy.

Another reason for speaking to every customer who enters is to warn potential shoplifters that they are noticed and that your eye is on them as they move around the displays.

Try to learn the names of customers who stop in regularly. Nothing makes a person feel more welcome than being greeted by name. Introduce yourself by name also, so you become somebody special to them, not just the person behind the counter. As you get to know your "regulars," you can begin to shop personally for them, spotting items, sending notes about specials. The legendary buyer, Jo Hughes built a career doing this at Bergdorf Goodman; her customers eventually referred to themselves as "Jo's girls."

In a very real sense, personal service is the main thing a small shop has to offer. True, you might be making much of your own inventory and carefully hand-picking the rest to offer your customers a merchandise mix the likes of which they've never seen. But the retailing giants who are your competitors are offering the same customers a gigantic selection of wares, often with vast price cuts and revolving credit plans, layaway arrangements, and periodic clearaways. As long as you compete against them with the magic of personal service, you'll stand to win every time.

If your shop's decor permits, try to include a community bulletin board. Become a regular stop for everybody who has a poster to put up or kittens to give away. Work to establish your store as a viable, caring part of your community. Also, if your budget is too limited to permit donations to every worthy cause, offer the use of your bulletin board as your contribution. It helps, and it works.

In retailing jargon, events that bring people into your shop are called "traffic builders." Time-honored ones are the Santa at Christmas time, and the free demonstration or sample giveaways. The idea behind traffic builders is based on the strength of numbers—the more people that trek through your store, the higher your chances are for sales.

One of the funniest traffic-builder stories is told by Ben Rosenthal, of the Small Business Administration's Service Core of Retired Executives. He tells of a shop he and some partners opened in a small town in Texas during the Depression, with no pre-opening promotion budget, and a slim purse to carry them through the beginning months.

They needed a terrific promotion to kick it all off, and he was very worried.

They finally took stock of the town and discovered that the townspeople were very religious. Every other block seemed to have a church in it, and attendance at services was high. This gave them their big idea. The store owners put all their excess efforts into building a big grandstand directly in front of the shop. Then they went around to every church they could find and announced that they were sponsoring a singing contest between the town's many church choirs.

The churches responded enthusiastically, and the store owners proceeded to the local newspaper office with a written notice of the contest, the names of the participating churches and the hours each choir was set to appear—coinciding, of course, with the opening week of the store. The clincher was that the winning choir would be selected by votes cast by the community. Anybody who wanted to vote was eligible, and the ballot box was placed inside the store.

The newspaper ran several major articles about the big contest. Religious leaders announced it from every pulpit in the town. Extra choir practice sessions were scheduled, special programs were prepared, and the entire network of church communication carried news of the big competition—and at the same time, news of the new store.

Obviously, the event was a smash. The store swarmed with voters who soon became customers, the store owners had generated untold waves of good will, "certificates of excellence" were awarded to some of the choirs, and the newspaper circulation increased. Rosenthal finishes his story by pointing out that the cost was virtually nil—they disassembled the grandstand and eventually used the wood for other purposes!

"Loss leaders" are another retailing phenomenon to

build traffic. A loss leader is some type of merchandise, usually in demand, that is offered at an amazingly low price in order to lure shoppers into the store. Loss leaders are heavily used in food marketing, with grocery stores running ads that list great savings, often limiting the purchases to one to a customer or "only available with a coupon clipped out of the ad." "Two for the price of one" is another loss-leader category.

The public relations effect of loss leaders is debatable. Whether the offering is made through advertising or by signs in the store window, a price-cutting image is one that a small store will do well to avoid. Almost any sizable, competitive store can offer more sales at lower prices than you can, so why play if you can't win?

Also, customers fast become used to big discount events and begin to schedule their shopping forays to coincide with price cuts, disrupting their drop-in-and-see-what's-new shopping habit. The browsing customer who enjoys your store will be a steady source of income. Let the bargain hunters go elsewhere if you're not prepared to discount heavily.

After you have made sure your store is groomed to be the most popular spot on the block, it's time to make up your own publicity calendar. Publicity, like advertising, is only as good as it is repetitive. A one-shot effort will get you nowhere. If you can't see your way clear to plan and carry out regularly scheduled activities, you'd be better off scrapping the whole thing for the first year or so and depending on favorable word-of-mouth publicity.

Most new retailers find that they do have the time and focus to do regular publicity as soon as the shop is open and functioning. The hectic pre-opening chaos passes, and the new-found quiet hours are ideal for publicity work based on your pre-planned calendar of events.

This by-the-month schedule of publicity and promotion

efforts is one of the first things a professional publicity organization does for a retail client. The calendar is based on the concept that retailing is a "special-events business." A steady stream of interesting happenings is necessary to speed up the repeat business cycle and to make the shop an exciting place to visit. Pre-planning the special events gives you much more control overall, and may save you money if you can reuse elements from separate promotions.

Begin by buying a large calendar that lists every holiday known to Western man. Some will be obvious. You know Chanukah/Christmas/New Year's Eve will be a wingding, as will Easter/springtime/Passover. Write in the calendar all the local events you can ferret out, such as your town's Founder's Day, local saints' celebrations, the town high school graduation, the library fair—any event that makes one day more special than another.

Add notes about seasonal activities. People usually go on vacations during summer months, they garden heavily in the spring, and they paint and fix up their homes and themselves more in the autumn than in other seasons, except possibly January, after their New Year's resolutions. Gather as many facts as you can about what makes up the extracurricular parts of every year. The more you get, the more chances you will have to include your shop in the merriment and also make more money.

Set your calendar aside and make a list of promotion activities and publicity outlets that are available to you. You might begin with distribution of handbills, which is a sure-fire, low-budget way of attracting customers to a special event. These can be mimeographed or photocopied and distributed by your own or other people's children, who are always looking for ways to earn extra money.

Include involvement at all local festivities. If there are competitions where prizes are donated by merchants, make note of them. The Chamber of Commerce often has a list of planned events, sponsorships of local teams, awards, and more that you could include.

Then set up your own press file. Drop by your library and make a list of every daily and weekly newspaper, magazine, newsletter, radio station and television station within a fifty-mile radius of your shop. Include complete address, zip code and phone number with area code. Then start reading and listening to each of your listings to pinpoint the name and style of the editor or broadcaster who handles stories about local people doing interesting things.

Every publication and every broadcast medium has such a person. The publications often place the editor in the "Women/Family/Home" section, while the broadcasters usually conduct daytime interview shows featuring local guests. Become familiar with their work, notice how they capture your attention, how they make their subjects sparkle. They are the people you will be contacting on a regular basis for publicity for your shop. Add their names to your press list.

Your first contact with the press people will be to introduce yourself to them and tell them what you are doing. Your contacts, from then on, will be to keep them updated on the interesting special events you are creating or participating in.

Your chances of getting written up or talked about depend on the timing, the competition, the news value and your presentation of the facts. These are a lot of variables. Your story might be super and still get rejected for any of the other reasons beyond your control. However, each time you give information to the press, you are building up an image for your shop as being an exciting, event-oriented place that is involved with the community. Again, repetitiveness is all-important.

The manner in which you present your story *is* within

your control. Nonwriters, take heart; you're just telling somebody what you're doing, the same as you would tell a friend on the telephone. You want it to be interesting, amusing and factual, with accurate times and dates. You do all this all the time with your friends, and now you can do it with the media.

News stories—i.e., professional publicity releases—all follow one pattern. They are written "from the top down," with the pertinent data included in the first few sentences, trailing off into less important information as the story proceeds. Each sentence should be written so that it could serve as the final sentence of the story if necessary. This is done so that the story can be cut easily from the bottom to fit into whatever space or time is available without losing the vital facts.

Actually, writing from the top down dates back to the Civil War, when newspaper federations such as the Associated Press used the telegraph to file stories. During the War the opposing armies cut the enemy's telegraph lines as often as possible. Reporters adjusted to the situation by giving all the facts in the first few sentences in case the rest of the transmission didn't get through.

Publicity items, which, oddly enough, make up the major portion of media space and time, are totally dependent on the real news of the day. If something earthshaking occurs at the last minute, everything scheduled for that issue or that broadcast is condensed a bit, and moved over to make room for the hot news item. So it's important that everything you send to the media can be easily condensed. Your chances for becoming a regular source of information for your press list depend on how usable your releases are.

As easy guide to writing "from the top down" is to make a list of the following: Who, What, Where, When, Why and How.

Now just fill in the answers and use it for the first few sentences of your release. The facts don't always have to be in this order, but all must be covered to give a total news picture. After you get the essentials in, go back and elaborate on whichever seem most pertinent, starting with the most important, and ending with the nonessentials. Press releases should be limited to one-page, typewritten, double-spaced.

Try to make your news sound fascinating so that the recipient will be intrigued and charmed. Check back and see what made the people and events sound so special in the material you researched when you were locating names for your press list. For instance, if you notice that a certain editor always likes to start a story with a funny anecdote, doesn't it make sense to include one high up in your release?

Photographs are occasionally attached to press releases, but are not necessary unless the release is about a certain item that just begs to be shown. Photographs for reproduction must be professional 8″ × 10″ glossy prints, skillfully lighted. These are expensive and are best avoided unless you are specifically requested to include a photograph. Sometimes papers will send their own photographer out to cover a story, so dicker if you have an editor interested in something visual and you don't have the budget to do it yourself.

If you do use photographs as part of the press release, type out identification of the picture plus your name, address and phone number and glue it on the back of the print. Then if it gets separated from the written story it can still be identified and used. Protect the front of the print with an extra piece of paper. If it gets scratched or marred it is unusable. *Never* write anything on the back of a print that's slated for reproduction, because the pencil or pen marks come through and damage the surface. If you mail prints, use cardboard stiffeners, never use paper clips. Be sure to address the envelope before you put the print in to prevent surface damage.

When contacting the media, recognize that they are all competing with each other, so your chances of getting write-ups regularly from everybody are pretty slim. Big-city newspapers often allocate less space to interesting local events than smaller or weekly papers do. The big broadcasters carry more network shows than the small independents. Since you are most interested in attracting the attention of potential customers, you want the most *local* media on a regular basis.

If you can schedule it, make your pre-opening publicity gesture a personal one. Write a one-page release, following the above instructions, telling who you are and why you're opening this type of shop in this location at this time. Make enough copies for everybody on your press list, and drop them off yourself at the local papers and stations. Try to meet the editor/broadcaster you've singled out as being right for you. Skip the personal approach for the media giants—just mail the releases to the attention of the person you've selected.

When you're at the paper or station, ask for the deadline times for your type of material. Sometimes a few hours make the difference between getting in and being rejected. Also, while you're there, ask for information about their advertising rates and schedule, so you can include them in future planning. Media people are always making a big point that their editorial staff is not influenced by their advertising sales, but it never hurts to mix the two, at least in your inquiries.

Now that you've got some idea of how to do it, go back to your publicity calendar and zero in on some events you know you will want to make a fuss over. Spread them around the calendar so you'll have something good hap-

pening every month. Your list probably will include some
of the following:

1: *September/October*
      Back to School
      Fall Fix-Up-Your-Home
      Halloween

2: *November/December*
      Thanksgiving
      Election Day
      Christmas
      Chanukah/Succoth
      New Year's Eve

3: *January/February/March*
      Lincoln's and Washington's Birthdays
      Valentine's Day
      St. Patrick's Day
      Groundhog Day
      Lent/Mardi Gras
      Martin Luther King Day
      Traditional sale time: markdowns,
        clearaway for spring-summer
        merchandise

4: *April/May/June*
      Spring
      Easter
      Passover
      Memorial Day
      Father's and Mother's Days
      Fix Up Your Home for Warm Weather
      Weddings
      Graduations

5: *July/August*
> Fourth of July
> Go on Vacation
> Dog Days
> Women's Suffrage Day
> Traditional sale time, clearaway
> for fall merchandise

Once you've selected a few events you want to promote, begin a file on each of them, collecting ideas on how you can make your promotion different and better than everybody else's. Involve local community groups wherever possible. Advance planning really works for publicity; as soon as you know what your promotion schedule is, you can start picking up or reserving parts of it. You need to tie everything in—ads, publicity, handbills and window and interior display. Go all out! Follow this pattern for each of your events, varying them from year to year. Know your schedule for the press, use everything within your reach, and work toward making each event really special and different.

For example, if you plan to put up a Christmas tree, you might send notes out in late October to senior citizens' groups, Girl Scout troops and after-school centers offering to display their handmade ornaments on your tree. If any group accepts, you've got a ready-made event to publicize.

Schedule the tree trimming for your slowest day in early December, and invite the group over. Access to a Polaroid camera helps here; everybody likes to have their picture taken, and you'll look as though you are doing something extra special for them. Also, if they take the pictures home and show them around, it extends your own publicity efforts.

Ten days before the tree trimming, send out your news release to all the people on your press list. Use a lot of the participants' names, spelled correctly. Supply extra copies of the release to the group in case they are friendly with any editors or have their own newsletter.

The Saturday following the tree trimming, get kids out to distribute handbills inviting people on the street to come see the ornaments by the community group. Put copies of the handbill up on community bulletin boards, and tack them on telephone poles in areas where this is permitted.

If your press release is picked up and run in any newspaper or magazine, get a reprint, and mount it, along with the front page masthead of the paper, and put it in the front window of the shop. Then write thank-you notes to the editor and the community group—and begin to think about your next month's promotion!

12

Alternative Selling Areas

It's hard to judge what merchandise mix will be best for any given shop. Even franchise operations, with pre-tested, sure-fire formulas do not thrive in every location. The first year or two in a new place is the time for re-evaluating and rebalancing both the stock and the concepts you started out with, reaching for a settled group of merchandise categories you know from experience your customers are seeking. Be ready to toss out whatever proves to be dead wood no matter how much you personally favor it.

By discarding, you make room in your shop and in your head for ventures into new categories, alternative selling areas that small retailers find are steady supplementary money makers. These alternatives fall into two groups—ones you can do within the shop, and ones you can do as outreach programs within the community, or to a larger audience by using the mail.

An easy-to-do alternative within the shop is the addition of "care" products related to the regular stock. For example, a leather shop can add a group of leather soaps, polishes, dyes, brushes and waterproofing sprays. A gift shop or jewelry store can carry a group of silver- and glass-polishing products and tarnish-resistant storage items, thus picking up added sales with little effort.

Another version of the care-products alternative is the addition of "our own" care products—concoctions based on standard products decanted, augmented and relabeled by the shop owners. These offer higher markup possibilities and tend to give the shop a class image if done attractively. Often scenting mass-market items with a drop or two of essential oils converts them into "our own." Test carefully, spend a bit of money on the packaging, and it will pay off.

Be sure that any added impulse items reflect the image of your shop, upholding the sense of quality and specialness you are trying to promote. Mass-produced, low-priced products that can be found in the local discount center will be detrimental. For example, plastic rain bonnets in their grisly little cases have no place in a "designed-just-for-you" boutique. However, if you sense there would be a market for plastic rain bonnets, get somebody to sew or crochet wonderful containers for them and set a basket out as an impulse item. It's the same idea of making everything in the shop special—and it works.

Printed materials are another good alternative selling area. Much depends on knowing your customer profile, and selecting books, prints, historical tracts or recipe cards that would tie in with your ideal customer's extended interests. Old photographs, picture postcards and ancient greeting cards are fascinating to many people, as are Victorian fashion plates, pattern reprints from *Godey's Lady's Book* or snips of old laces and ribbons suitable for framing.

Museums are often good sources for interesting printed material. An outstanding collection is published by the Greenfield Village and Henry Ford Museum, Dearborn,

Michigan, with such charmers as the *Discriptive Catalogue of E. S. Frost & Co.'s Hooked Rug Patterns*, originally sold in the 1870s. The Museum of Fine Arts in Boston offers, among other delights, a pattern book for a Biblical appliqué quilt originally made by "Harriet Powers, a Negro woman, in Athens, Georgia, probably between 1895 and 1898."

For craft galleries and hobby shops, a common alternative selling area is the skills class given by the shop owner or by a local expert. Doubly advantageous, the course brings extra traffic into the shop on off-peak hours and educates future customers for materials and for purchase of gallery pieces. When outside experts are brought in to teach a course, care must be taken to establish the ground rules between you and the teacher. Draw up a simple contract in letter form so each of you is familiar with the expectations of the other.

There are several arrangements that are commonly used for teaching or giving lessons:

1. You and the teacher agree on the number of students needed to conduct the course. Both of you advertise and/or publicize, splitting the expenses of mailings, etc. You both take an equal share of the course tuition money. You make extra money by selling the craft supplies but have the added expense of the shop overhead.

2. You both agree on the minimum number of students. You do all the publicizing/advertising. The instructor is paid a flat fee per session regardless of how many students there are. Fees vary but usually range between $35 and $50 a lecture. If the minimum number of students don't sign up, the whole arrangement is canceled.

3. The teacher sets up the entire course, handles all the expenses and keeps all the tuition money. You furnish only the meeting place and sell the students their materials. With this arrangement there are seldom minimums set on the number of students.

As long as you are not hiring the instructor on a permanent, full-time basis, she is considered a free-lance worker, and no tax or compensation/disability enters into your agreement.

Boutiques selling apparel have access to additional alternative selling methods through alteration services and customer-order items. A good, fast alteration service can be a rent-payer in that it helps bind the customers to the shop. They know they will look good in anything they take home with them and it simplifies their lives. Include the fact that an alteration service is part of your shop in any publicity or advertising you do. It's a good selling point.

Alteration prices should be in line with what other quality shops in the area are charging, or slightly higher than those charged by the local tailor or dressmaker. Alteration work, since it is sporadic, is often farmed out to local home sewers, who follow the pinnings and markings of the shop owner.

Custom-order apparel is a different story. It works only if you are already producing a lot of your own merchandise and thus have the expertise, materials and equipment on hand.

Pricing custom-order work varies with the type of job. For example, if you have the size, pattern and fabric in the shop, a surcharge of 5 to 10 percent over the normal ready-made price is usual. If the customer furnishes her own fabric, in a weight similar to that you are accustomed to working with, a 5 percent overcharge is common. Most shops charge extra for anything requiring extra work—a fabric of much different weight requiring pattern adjustment, style changes in any portion of the garment or different trimmings.

The first fitting of a custom-order garment is always included in the quoted price, but there is often an additional charge for subsequent fittings, ranging between $5 and $10. Whatever your fitting policy is, make sure the customer is aware of it before you and she move past the talking stage. It may seem harsh to levy extra charges on fittings, but custom-order shops have found it is a good way to speed up the flow of work and therefore the flow of money.

The serving of food and beverages is another favorite alternative selling method. It is an outgrowth of the "make the shop a lovely place to spend time in" philosophy, and it is surprisingly successful when it works. However, shop owners who have combined a coffeehouse with selling merchandise caution that a different pace is needed to make the whole thing operative. Less in-depth stocking of merchandise is called for, plus much faster introduction of new items, and banishing of nonsellers. It is crucial that the regular patrons who drop in often somehow never get the feeling they have seen everything in the shop before. Obviously you can't restock each week, but there must be constant rearrangement of the displays, daily overhaul of the high-visibility areas and a steady trickle of brand-new items that can be spread around the shop to perk up existing stock. If the pace is allowed to slow down, sales fall off immediately, and the retail end of the business becomes secondary to the serving of food.

Adding a café also means a gigantic amount of extra work, requires special licensing, and can seldom all be handled by one person. Most often the food-and-beverage area is given out to another person as sort of a franchise within the main shop. This has the advantage of bringing lots of extra traffic in, creating a setting for special events and adding to the publicity possibilities.

Financial arrangements between the shop owner and the food person can be whatever both want to make them. Most often there is some method set up to combine overhead expenses—rent, heat, light and cleaning services. This arrangement usually is made in relationship to the break-even point of the food operation, with a set percentage being taken of the net profit and applied to overhead bills. Whatever arrangement you decide upon, spell it out in simple letter form so both of you can fully understand what is expected of each.

If the food person is not an experienced restauranteur, suggest that he or she send for the Small Business Administration book *Starting and Managing a Small Restaurant*, Catalog number SBA 1.15:9. It costs under $2 and is a terrific resource, containing eminently usable hard facts.

For apparel stores, the most common alternative selling method operating either inside or outside the shop is the fashion show. Showing garments on the right people is a never-fail promotion method! If you have your own food service area, be sure to schedule informal modeling during luncheon or tea time or whatever your peak hours are. Supply the model with the necessary selling information and encourage an informal atmosphere so the customers will ask questions.

Fashion shows done outside the shop become major promotional events, especially if they are tied in with a community group or some local festivity. Invite the club members or local women active in community affairs to be your models. Women tend to want to buy the clothing they have modeled in a show. This can be encouraged by offering the models a discount on the fashions they have modeled.

Don't plan a long show—45 minutes is plenty, presenting between twenty and thirty outfits. Know who your audience will be—what age and what income bracket they will represent—and design the show to tempt them. Accessorize each outfit as completely as you can, and show as many related garments as possible. This adds excitement to the presentation, with models appearing muffled up in coats and scarfs, then slipping out of them to show surprises underneath.

Background music is an absolute necessity for a show. Use tapes to put together a selection reflecting the show. For example, if you are showing summer clothes, tape appropriate music such as "Heat Wave," "Summertime," "Take Me Out to the Ball Game" and "Too Darn Hot." Your life will be simpler if you tape music with a strong, regular beat so the models will have a definite rhythm to walk to. In lieu of tapes, find LP records that have a mix of fast and slow tunes so the show will have a varied pace.

Somebody has to be the commentator for a fashion show, pointing out the style facts of each outfit. Since you bought the clothes and know the market trends, the logical commentator is you—no matter how nonverbal you might feel about it. There are only two considerations for the commentator: (1) keep it informal; (2) keep it brief.

A way to guarantee both of these rules is to write four or five key words for each outfit on small index cards and use them as the basis for your statements. Avoid writing out complete sentences. They don't allow you freedom of invention and always sound static when read. On the other hand, never try to speak without any notes unless you are a true pro.

You need at least three people to run a show: two backstage to supervise the clothes and accessories changes, and one out front giving the commentary. Don't overload the backstage crew. If you're well organized, you won't need extra people who tend to become noisy. Silence must be the rule for backstage.

The show will run most smoothly if each outfit is set up well in advance. Hang each garment on a hanger and put all the accessories that go with it, including shoes, hose and jewelry, into a shopping bag. Write on the bag the model's name and her position in the show, hang the bag around the hanger, and you're ready to go! Organize the changing room before the models arrive, establishing a place for each person, with enough shelf, chair and table space to accommodate quick changes.

Give each model a card to carry on the runway with the price of the outfit lettered on it. Check the visibility of the cards before the show; if the customers can't see the price, they're less likely to buy. If this is unacceptable to your models, make up a mimeographed price list following the exact order of the show, and put a copy on each chair before the audience arrives.

The thing to bear in mind is that you are furnishing entertainment. (Avoid using babies or animals for effect—they're too unreliable.) Plan the show in a logical order, beginning with low-key costumes, and building to a smashing finale. The French couture designers always end their collections with a wedding gown. You don't have to go that far, but aim to leave your audience cheering!

Ask your models to arrive two hours before show time so you can run through the entire presentation. Do a complete dress rehearsal with the music, the lighting, if any, and all the accessories, exactly following the plan for the show. Take it very slow and allow everybody to become familiar with their parts. Stress that you must speed everything up for the audience, but stroll through the rehearsal to cut tension.

If you want to spend the extra money, supply the audience with little favors (something with the shop's name on it, perhaps) and have the models pass them out as part of the finale. However, select something that reflects your store image. A single fresh daffodil or a Christmas candy cane will do more for your "specialness" than dreary ballpoint pens with your name printed on them.

Fashion shows are often great tie-ins with organizations that need to raise funds. If you find you can do a good fashion show without wiping out the rest of your responsibilities for the month, send little notes around to groups offering them a fashion show as the focus for their fund raising. They supply the place and the models and sell admission tickets. You supply the show entertainment and reap the sales. Again, clearly spell out all arrangements in a letter so everybody will know what is expected of them.

Trunk shows are another alternative selling method, similar to fashion shows but applicable to many other types of merchandise. With trunk shows you go out into the community, present a selection of goodies from your regular stock and do the selling on the spot. Again, community organizations and church groups are logical choices to offer your trunk show to; they supply the place and the audience, you supply the entertainment. If you want to offer a trunk show as a fund raiser to groups, give the organization a small percentage of the profits made from the presentation.

Select trunk-show merchandise with an eye to sprightly commentary, make up your own cue cards, organize the packaging of the show, and you're ready to tour the provinces. People buy more when they are told fascinating tidbits about the products, letting them in on behind-the-scenes information. Have prices clearly marked, and remember to bring sales slips and wrapping materials. These are all retail sales, so state tax requirements must be met.

Block parties, street fairs and outdoor markets are versions of the trunk show. At these events you seldom get a chance to present any sort of focused commentary, and you will be competing for the customer's dollar with everybody else in the area. However, the potential audience is much larger than at a closed gathering, so your profit possibilities are greater.

Fees for these events vary widely, depending on the size and sophistication of the sponsoring group. Expect to pay something, however, for your right to be in the show. Advance promotion is covered by your entry fee, so check out what is planned. The entrance money usually goes for the bare space *only*; find out if you must supply your own table and chairs, and bring your own display materials. Occasionally the fee includes a catalogue listing if one is published.

The only realistic way to scout out the money-making potential of fairs is to attend them as a spectator, get a clear idea of what merchandise is selling well, and talk to as many of the exhibitors as possible. Base your decision on as many facts as you can gather.

Notice, too, which displays attract the most notice. The importance of your display cannot be overemphasized; it will make the difference between sales and no sales. The problem is one of engineering. The display must be portable and easily cleaned, have some provision for lofting a sign or banner, have a skirt covering storage space beneath the counter and be uncluttered enough to furnish an attractive neutral background for the stock.

Business cards are a must at outside selling events. Offer them to everybody that seems interested, letting them know you have a whole shop filled with exciting items rather than just those shown at the fair. If you have any catalogues, handbills or mailing pieces, put them out, too.

Use the show to build up a mailing list of satisfied customers. Each time you sell something, get the buyer's name and address on the sales slip. After the event get the data from your carbon copies so you can mail out news of sales and special events in the shop. When making out sales slips, remember that fairs and markets are still retail selling, and tax requirements must be met.

An increasing number of shop owners extend their customer audience through catalog sales and/or direct-mail selling. Both require additional capital far beyond that needed for the other alternative selling areas discussed in this chapter. Designing, producing and distributing a creditable catalogue can cost hundreds of dollars. On the other hand, getting out a simple black-and-white one-page flier can often be done in quantities of 1000 for under $100. As with most promotions, repetition is the key to success, so a budget of $500 for a series of fliers would not be out of line.

Bea Baron, proprietor of Beahive Enterprises, a feminist mail-order business, says the first step toward looking into mail-order selling is to sketch out the kind of flier you're interested in. Use standard-weight paper, either 8½″ × 11″ or legal size, and make a dummy copy of the finished product, drawing lines where you want the descriptions, and blocking out spaces to indicate where the artwork is to be placed.

If you expect returns by mail, include an ordering coupon set aside from the rest of the material by heavy dotted lines; put spaces on the coupon for all the information you need to know to fill an order. Include your shop name and complete address on the coupon itself. If you do not expect orders by mail, Bea feels it is a good practice to include a discount coupon offering a lower price on some item if the customer brings the mailer back to the shop. It not only brings in some extra business, it also helps you decide whether or not you are wasting your money sending out the fliers.

Work to make the dummy as representative as you can of the look and style of the shop. Use a typeface similar to the one used on your sign, banner, inside display signs or shopping bags. Reinforce your own image. Become aware of the mailing pieces you receive, and notice what makes one more attractive than another. Experiment with designing a self-mailer that can be folded back into itself and does not require an envelope.

Once you've got what you think you want, take it to several printers for estimates. Be prepared to answer the following:

- Number of copies needed
- Size, color(s) of ink and of paper
- Type of artwork (line drawing is less expensive than photography)
- Source of artwork—you, the printer or the photographer
- Time available in which to do the job
- Any folding, collating or stapling needed
- Mailing restrictions, if you are trying to keep the finished product under a certain number of ounces

Compare estimates and compare samples of each printer's work. If your shop sells quality, your mailers must look quality. It usually helps to confess to the printer that this is your maiden venture into mail-order selling and to depend on them to come up with suggestions to simplify the entire process.

After conferring with the printers, take the dummy mailer to your local post office and find out exactly how much postage each piece will require and what arrangements you would have to make to keep the post office happy with the size mailings you plan. Post offices are federally run, but each one seems to have its own game plan. Since mail service is crucial to the success of the operation, be sure you know what is expected of you.

If you plan four or five mailings of a thousand pieces each year, it might be to your advantage to get a bulk mailing permit. This is for a special kind of mailing where you do some of the preliminary work for the post office, and thus get a lower postage rate per item. For example, the current first-class rate is 5 cents for one once of mail. The bulk rate is 8.4 cents per piece not to exceed 3.7 ounces. Quite a difference!

The bulk mailing permit is issued to you for use in one post office only, and the preliminary work you must do consists of having every piece zip-coded and then sorted out into separate bundles, one bundle per zip code. Bulk mailings are supposedly scheduled for slower service than first-class mail, but the actual speed of delivery seems to depend a great deal on the location and work load of the local post office.

The cost of the bulk mailing is what makes it feasible for larger periodic mailings. There is a one-time fee of $15 for the permit number, usable for the life of your mailing program. Then there is an additional charge of $40 per year for the yearly permit. You really have to figure out how much money you would save after deducting the initial investment.

There are a few other postal facts that you should know:

First-class mail   May be sealed; will be forwarded to a new address or returned to the sender if unclaimed. Most

	expensive way of mailing anything.
Third- or fourth-class mail	Will not be forwarded or returned unless the sender indicates she will cover the additional postage charges by writing on the mailer "Return Postage Guaranteed" or "Forwarding and Return Postage Guaranteed." Costs less than first-class mail.
Address correction	The sender can write "Address Correction Requested" on the mailing piece, and she will receive the address to which the mail was forwarded or will be told the reason why the letter could not be delivered. Since this is pretty involved, there is an extra charge per correction request. This service is available on first-, third- and fourth-class mail.

While you are at the post office be sure to register your business name with them if you are doing business under anything other than your own name. Make sure any mail that arrives with your business name on it will be delivered to you.

After you've gotten the flier and postal information settled, you have to figure out who you're going to mail to. The best, most responsive mailing list is, of course, the one you put together yourself from all the names and addresses on your sales slips. These are people who have obviously been pleased with your merchandise and are most likely to buy again. Keep a guest book out in your shop to collect additional names from those who didn't buy but who like the kind of thing you sell.

If you don't have enough of your own names to make up a mailer, you can borrow or rent mailing lists from local organizations, other noncompetitive businesses, school alumni associations and so forth. Once you get away from your own customer list, the response will generally go down, but if the people on the lists are similar to your ideal customer profile, they are worth trying to reach.

Mailing lists may also be acquired from companies throughout the United States who make a business of furnishing lists. They usually have a minimum order and charge so much per name or per thousand names. Costs vary according to how specialized the names on the list are. For example, if you are trying to reach owners of pleasure boats in the state of Wisconsin, the list will cost you more than a list of retired persons in the Southwest.

Check the yellow pages of the largest cities near you to locate mailing list houses. There are any number of rental arrangements companies offer, from issuing you pre-addressed gummed labels to requiring you to furnish envelopes to the mailing house and paying them to address each one from their lists.

List companies insert some phony names into each mailing list to keep track of whether their list has been fraudulently duplicated. Their monitoring is careful and serious, so beware!

The percentage of response you can look for which a rented mailing list varies with how specialized the names are. Between 5 and 10 percent is suggested with highly selective lists, while 2 percent is considered a good return from a general set of names.

Direct mail done on a large scale is a complex operation for a small shop to venture into. Direct mail to past customers and local community group members can be a nice augmentation to daily sales. If you do decide to check into nonlocal selling, get the three pertinent booklets put out by the Small Business Administration: *Selling By Mail Order, National Mailing List House* and *National Directories for Use in Marketing*.

Additional information is available from the Direct Mail/Marketing Association, 6 East 43rd Street, New York, N.Y. 10017.

13

Art Galleries

"The first thing to understand when you're talking about galleries," says Warren Hadler, "is that there are two kinds. One is set up to lose money and the other is set up to make money."

Warren is co-owner of the newsmaking Hadler Galleries, with branches in New York, Houston, and a contract division that supplies works of art to museums, corporations and collectors all over the world. Warren adds, "We are set up to make money."

A gallery that is set up to lose money is also referred to as a vanity gallery or, in financial terms, a tax loss or tax shelter. Most often it is funded by high income persons hoping to show losses on their business investments in order to lower the amount of income tax they must pay. If the gallery is "successful" in it's intent it loses money every year, and allows the backers to lower their tax base. The worst thing that could happen to a tax shelter gallery is to show a profit because then it is no longer useful to it's backers.

The type or caliber of art shown in tax loss galleries may be similar to that featured in money making galleries, it's just the bottom line that's different. Or, the gallery may be available on a rental basis to anyone who wants to put on an art show.

As such, the tax loss gallery is dependent not only on functioning at a loss, it is also dependent on the financial health of the parent business. When the backers no longer need a tax write-off, i.e. the market goes down or money gets tight, the gallery is one of the first things to go, and another business failure is added to that year's statistics.

Serious gallery owners speak disparagingly about the vanity operations. They are described most often as an arrangement where a husband will set his wife up in a gallery. She might have been an art major back in college or have taken up painting as a hobby. When the children grow up she begins looking for something to do with her life. This coincides with his peak earning years so a tax loss looks like a fine idea. The gallery functions for a few years and then is closed down, leaving the woman with mixed feeling of relief and failure.

"Think twice" is the message here if someone offers to set you up in a tax loss gallery. The end results may outweigh the advantages.

Opening a gallery requires a philosophical decision months or even years before a location is selected. A deep commitment to art, coupled with in-depth knowledge of and experience with one clearly defined area are mandatory. The art field is elitist. If you have developed a depth of knowledge—know period, style, persons and values in that area—then all else is possible. You arrive at gallery openings with a working knowledge, an overview of values and transactions and a developed taste that no amount of hasty research can bring. It's all very personal, and much depends on where you are coming from.

Warren Hadler and his partner, Nicolas Rodriquez, see their gallery as an extension of the artists whose works they carry. Warren says, "The art of promoting is just as creative as other art forms. Presentation is 50% of selling. Galleries present works that artists are incapable of promoting themselves."

He compares contemporary art gallery owners to other promoters. Special persons promote special things; rock star managers do for their clients exactly what gallery owners do for their artists. In our culture art has a mystique and needs interpretation—that's where the gallery comes in. It presents works by generally nonverbal persons to a public who must be educated to "see" the object.

Another function of contemporary art galleries is to extend support to their artists, to tend them as it were, so they are able to develop and produce. This shepherding syndrome reinforces the need to be very knowledgeable in your area because you are backing a commodity that isn't even in existence at the time of support. Few galleries have the money to keep their artists on retainers, but most have arrangements whereby they loan small amounts against potential sales or buy early works. It all adds up to keeping the artists secure enough to work, an expense unique to contemporary galleries.

Galleries specializing in art works from the past escape the care and feeding of their artists, but must monitor the international art market closely. There are a limited number of items attributed to each artist. The successful gallery owner will know where each work is, what the current market value is, and be able to spot activities and sales as they are occurring. Again, this is not exactly a field that can be learned by quick research. Most of the legendary dealers grew up with art and have spent their lifetimes immersed in it.

The functional organization of a profitable gallery most often is divided into two divisions. One section is the operation of the gallery itself—planning and executing a certain number of shows per year. The other division contacts, presents and sells works to architects, interior designers, corporations, builders and museum directors. This division operates independently of the gallery space and, if successful, brings in steady, year-round income that helps offset the fluctuations of money from the exhibitions.

Most art sales are a one-time transaction. Even avid private collectors seldom can purchase enough to keep a gallery in business. By balancing the two sources of income the gallery owner has a better chance of achieving financial security and exerts more control over the fate of his artists. Although the two divisions are separate business enterprises they are interrelated in promoting one set of artists.

Time allocations become important when the gallery owner operates in both divisions. Working with architects and designers is a demanding job along with putting on four to six shows a year, nurturing the artists you already have, plus being available to find and develop new people. Yet few successful galleries can afford to sell through their exhibitions alone.

The logistics of setting up a gallery are similar to those of opening up any shop. Research comes first; know what and where your competition is. Learn who they exhibit and who their clients are. Attend their shows and figure out what you will be offering that is different and better. Observe their presentations and determine what works smoothly and why. Above all, select an art area that is not already covered. The art market is too small to stand much competition.

Location is more important to a gallery than a shop. Having the correct address is vital and to art buyers this usually means being in an expensive part of town. Don't bother with surveys of street traffic, people don't wander in off the street and purchase works of art.

Today art is status and your gallery must be one in which clients would expect to find beautiful, expensive things. Gallery owners reiterate: you must educate people into becoming your clients. You must get to know them intimately, get personally involved with every client and build up a feeling of trust so they are comfortable spending large sums of money in your gallery on things that will become a part of their lives.

Once you locate the best street to be on, preferably one on which other galleries are located, your concern shifts to the amount of renovation necessary to put the space into good working condition. Solid, plain walls; good, unobtrusive flooring and a ceiling that will house a movable lighting system are considered necessary for a gallery—and the fewer renovations, the better. Price out the renovations you see as necessary. Get estimates from workers, and verify references whenever possible. Aim toward creating a serene, well-lighted place that has flexibility. Track lighting is a must, as are wall materials that can be easily resurfaced.

Another plus that one space might have over another is the presence of security guards in the building. Insurance is an important part of a gallery's budget and the rates are sometimes lower if the building has twenty-four-hour security surveillance.

Gallery owners are divided as to their need for large amounts of storage space. Some opt for minimal space on the theory that everything in the gallery is for sale and needs to be on display. Others feel that storage space is a necessity so pieces can be constantly shifted around and interchanged to keep the gallery new looking. A little office space is called for; a filing cabinet and a slide file can house the architects' and designers' selling material.

A private meeting room is sometimes mentioned as a need for a gallery, however, many owners handle privacy with certain clients by arranging individual meetings on a day the gallery is closed to the public.

The three ways of setting up any business are the choices available to the potential gallery owner. The personal liability of the individual proprietorship or unincorporated partnership is sometimes an obstacle for a gallery dealing in high priced items. A corporation or an incorporated partnership are most often selected.

A growing trend among artists is to open cooperative galleries similar in structure to the cooperatives described in Chapter 5. Co-op members pay a yearly fee that covers the overhead, often including a director's salary. Show expenses are paid by the individuals whose work is exhibited. A separate publicity budget is sometimes set up and supported by all members. Few cooperative galleries charge any commission on sales. All members have a voice in the operation of the gallery and in the selection of new members.

Budgeting for a gallery is both similar and different from a retail shop. Overhead categories are the same:

> rent
> utilities
> telephone
> office expenses
> personnel
> cleaning service
> insurance
> advertising/promotion
> repairs and maintenance
> payroll taxes
> miscellaneous

Do the research necessary for you to make reasonably accurate estimates for overhead.

Once you have an idea of your monthly expenses you are ready to estimate what it will cost you to present your products, i.e. hold gallery exhibitions and make contacts with architects and designers. Here's where the big difference comes in, separating galleries from shops. You have no real inventory to draw from; each time you mount an exhibition you start from scratch.

Most galleries have four to six shows each year. The new gallery might stick to four: two spring shows (February/March and April/May) and two fall shows (September/October and November/December.) Summer is vacation time for galleries except those located in summer resort areas.

The cost per show can vary a bit. It can also be shared between gallery owner and artist. However, your planning will be aided if you select a rock bottom figure that gives you the kind of exhibition in keeping with the look and price level of the gallery. You are selling quality and status so beware of any tendency to skimp.

The cost per show budget should include:

> invitations
> mailing fees
> gallery renovations
> framing/mounting
> special display units
> opening party/refreshments/personnel
> publicity/advertising
> insurance

These are the costs that will happen four times a year and are independent of your monthly overhead. Warren Hadler estimates that the Hadler Gallery New York openings cost about two thousand dollars each.

His figures break down as follows:

> invitations—photograph—$250.00
> printing—$650.00
> mailing—$250.00
> restructuring the gallery—$250.00
> extra display units—$300.00
> opening party—$150.00
> miscellaneous—$150.00

He adds ruefully that each show is approached individually but somehow the amount always ends up near two thousand dollars, no matter what.

Invitations are a large part of the show budget. They are worth spending money on since the majority of the audience will base their decision to come or not to come by what they see on the mailer. A good, clear photograph of a representative work is mandatory and will be most effective if backed up with some concise, well-written biographical information. Few galleries can get away with a no-photograph invite unless the works being shown are so well known that the clientele needs no visualization.

The question of color versus black and white photographs always comes up. We live in a world of color; ideally all mailing pieces would feature beautiful color prints. If your budget allows, by all means use color, at least for the major show of your fall season. Be sure the color reproduction is spectacular enough to do justice to the mailing piece. Better a fine black and white picture than a color print of mediocre quality.

Printed exhibition catalogues are overlooked by most of the smaller galleries as a matter of economics. Unless the show is set to travel to other parts of the country, a catalog is an exhorbitant expense. The artist can document the show personally, as most do, so a record will exist if it is ever needed.

The word "insurance" appears on both the overhead

budget and the show budget because they cover separate circumstances. Standard, year round gallery insurance includes protection against fire, water damage, liability and theft. In addition, a short-term Fine Arts Floater can be added to a regular insurance policy to cover all risks while art works are in transit or on the premises of the gallery. Costs are in proportion to value of the art works, materials, distances, etc.

Almost no contemporary galleries buy works unless they are dealing with prints. Consignment is the norm for original art. This leaves gallery owners free to invest their money in promoting the shows and covering overhead. Consignment arrangements vary widely; the only point everybody seems to agree on is the need for a written contract spelling out the relationship between the artist and the gallery owner. The percentage split differs throughout the country; 60% to the artist and 40% to the gallery is most common, with many areas moving into a straight 50/50 split.

The financial arrangement is only a small part of the contract, and one that causes the least worry. Length of time, exclusivity, shipping and framing costs all can be stumbling blocks. Volunteer Lawyers for the Arts, a pioneer program arranging for free legal aid to artists has designed a model contract which is reprinted in the Appendix on page 216. VLA spokespersons suggest gallery owners use this contract as a basis, revising it to make the contract pertinent to individual needs.

Legalities of contracts between artists and galleries are under discussion in many parts of the United States, especially rulings on the resale of an artist's original work. A case in point is the artist Robert Indiana, whose "Love" design has been reproduced on everything from fabrics to costume jewelry with little financial gain for the artist.

A state law in California now requires payments to an

artist for resale of his works for as long as the artist lives. The law was greeted with enthusaism by some and is being questioned by many others. As it stands the law is predicated on every artist's work becoming more valuable, thus meriting a percentage fee each time the work changes hands. What is missing, of course, is a workable guideline for works of art that decrease in value; who bears the brunt of that?

Included in the Appendix on page 216 are names and addresses of countrywide groups affiliated with Volunteer Lawyers for the Arts, offering reference material and advice on arts-related law. The contract situation is in a state of transition and bears watching by gallery owners.

Back to budgeting. Once you have determined your overhead expenses and your cost per show, give some attention to the non-show selling you plan to do. Color slides are the standard way to show art work to architects and designers; building and maintaining a comprehensive slide library is a must. Artists may supply slides at their own expense, share the costs with you or you may choose to design and fund your own presentations.

The gallery must maintain prices when selling to architects and designers. If a piece is offered to private clients at a certain price, the exact same amount must be charged to corporate clients. Architects and art buyers representing major corporations or foundations rarely expect a fee or commission; however, smaller firms often expect a portion of the gallery's commission on works sold. The percentage of the split varies. If possible, check with other gallery owners who have done business with the firm and determine the amount of the fee split they paid.

Art buyers and art dealers who work independently generally take a percentage of the gallery's commission for their services. Again, amounts vary, so verify the arrangements with other gallery owners if you can. When selling in conjunction with another gallery, either to private or to corporate clients, expect to make an even 50/50 division of the gallery's commission money. This makes the sale relatively unprofitable but it's necessary if you want to spread your wings and be able to deal with clients in other parts of the world.

The more exposure you have, the better it is. Clients are highly mobile; architects and designers work in many locales, the art buying public travels extensively and often maintains several residences. Arrangements with other galleries benefit everybody. Such arrangements are rarely formalized, rather they are personal "understandings" between professionals.

Museum directors and government officials constitute another viable market. Federal legislation is establishing a percentage of the budget of each new government building that has to be spent on works of art. Here again, slides are your presentation medium, so keep an eye out for new building in your area.

Many gallery owners feel that architects and interior designers are an excellent starting point for a new gallery owner. They are easy to locate and have an active trade press so you can study the field before you make any contacts. Begin with the Yellow Pages of the nearest large city. In addition to company listings, many areas have an Architect's League or Association with a members directory. Credentialed designers belong to the National Society of Interior Designers which has chapters across the country—get names, call and make appointments.

Trade magazines worth following regularly include Interior Design Magazine, Residential Interiors, Contract Magazine, Architectural Digest and Progressive Architecture. Check the reference room of your local public library. From monthly readings of the publications you will develop a working knowledge of the field. Read to find out which firms are doing what kinds of work so your sales calls will have optimum effectiveness.

In budgeting your out-of-the-gallery selling try to estimate how much travel will be involved. Business travel is a tax deductible business expense but must be documented with receipts. The IRS Tax Guide for Small Business tells you all you need to know about travel deductions, and is yours for the asking at any IRS office.

To pull together all your costing figures and determine an approximate total for expenses in all three areas, add up:

Overhead—enough to carry you for three to six months

Gallery exhibits—two of your four shows

Non-gallery selling—presentation plus six months expenses

Compare the totals you come up with to the amount of art you would need to sell: first, enough to cover your expenses, and second, to operate at a profit you would be happy with. Knowledge of the field is a necessity here. If you know your area and the customer potential you can make a reasonable guess. Then check your totals against the floor space available to you. Is there enough room to house the size operation you will need to ensure the volume you want?

Gallery owners advise newcomers to do some selling before they actually set up their own place. Six months spent dealing from your home or working in somebody else's gallery will give you a better feeling for cash flow than all the estimates in the world. Try to experience both private clients and selling trips to architects. You need to operate in both areas to make the gallery work.

Warren Hadler gave a great illustration of the need to balance the operation during a recent show at his New York Gallery. The costs had once again come out to about two thousand dollars. Only one sale was made during the exhibition—an eight hundred dollar piece. The show was excellent and the artist very talented, but the money hadn't come in. The balancing of the Hadler business removed the pressure; Warren had sold eight thousand dollars worth of tapestries to a museum director the day before the show closed.

If there is one factor that determines the success or failure of an art gallery it is the publicity and promotion that goes into it. (See Chapter 9.) Some galleries advertise, some do not. If your budget allows, pattern your initial year's advertising after that of the other galleries in your area.

Also extremely important is public relations. The relationship between gallery owner and client is unique and very personal. Retailers can function with a pleasant, surface relationship between them and their customers. A gallery operator needs to build a mystique, become a trusted friend and recognized authority, and make the gallery the "in" place.

Major galleries have full time public relations people keeping their name in front of the public, insuring high visibility in all the right places. Smaller galleries have to do it themselves. "Think Total Commitment," the newcomer is advised. Operating a gallery is a whole life style devoted to being out there and being visible. All social commitments are generally gallery oriented. This presents problems to anyone who has family responsibilities or a schedule that prohibits mobility. Success of a gallery is in direct proportion to what you put into it. The decision is up to you.

14

Some Successful Ventures and Why They Worked

Going on to bigger, better and more lucrative ventures is the expected aim of most new business persons. However, astonishingly high failure rates for retailing indicate a need to know how to go about dissolving a business. Suppose you give it the old school try, but end up feeling you would be happier in some other work area. You are financially solvent, but want out.

As an individual proprietor or a simple partnership, you can go out of business by selling all of your assets, including patents, copyrights and goodwill, to anybody who wants to buy and at any price you both agree on. If after computing the value of the assets you end up making money on the sale, the gain will be taxed as ordinary income. Conversely, a loss in money will be treated as a business loss on your personal income tax.

If no buyers are found for your business you can simply close up by getting rid of all the assets, and dealing with the profit or loss on your personal tax return.

Things are more complicated for a corporation. A corporation may close up by disposing of its assets for cash and then distributing the cash to its stockholders, or it may just distribute its assets direct to the stockholders in exchange for their shares of stock. The liquidating of a corporation must be conducted according to various IRS rules and procedures, and should be handled by an attorney or accountant.

On the other hand, suppose you are not making it financially. You not only want out, but the creditors are at your door. "Bankruptcy" is the word, and the process is not all that grim.

In this country bankruptcy proceedings are an orderly way to get everybody concerned out of a negative situation with as little damage as possible. Iris Bragin, Supervisor of the Bankruptcy Clerk's Office, Southern District, New York, sums it up: "Bankruptcy is a privilege, not a right." If the procedure is followed accurately and in good faith, the persons involved will be making the best out of a sad thing.

The psychological damage to most people hinges on how much of their identity is tied up in the business. To some, to fail in business means to fail as a human being. No amount of rational proceedings can change this inner attitude.

Bankruptcy laws are federal laws, part of the federal court system, which divides the United States into geographic divisions. The basic rules apply to everybody in the country, with additional regulations added on by individual states. The additions generally deal with property-exemption laws, which are under the jurisdiction of each state.

Individuals and unincorporated partnerships can file for bankruptcy without the services of a lawyer. Corporations must be represented by an attorney. The amount of money an attorney plans to charge for handling a bankruptcy case is reviewed by the court, as is the projected method of payment, and may be changed by the judge if anything seems out of line.

The fee to file for any type of bankruptcy is $50. This may be paid in installments if you file an application asking the judge to grant you this privilege. The usual installment arrangement is to divide the fee in half, paying one-half about 30 days after the first court meeting and the second half about 30 days later. Payment of the filing fee is important—the proceeding cannot be brought to a close if the fee is outstanding.

The two types of bankruptcy that pertain to small businesses are:

Chapter Four:	Straight bankruptcy, where there is no possible way the business could be pulled together and reorganized in order to operate profitably.
Chapter Eleven:	A partial bankruptcy, which can be filed only if the business is *not* in hopeless condition. Under Chapter Eleven the business is given another chance to become profitable. If you decide to try for a Chapter Eleven bankruptcy, you must be prepared to show how and why you expect the business to recover.

Both types of bankruptcy are filed for with forms that come in kits published by Julius Blumberg, Inc., available at legal stationers throughout the country. Specify which of the Blumberg Bankruptcy kits you want—Chapter Four or Chapter Eleven. Both are priced inexpensively and contain enough sets of each page to satisfy requirements, plus instructions, worksheets, envelopes and heavy covers.

The kits cover everything. For example, the Chapter Four (straight bankruptcy) begins with the Voluntary Petition, in which you identify yourself as being qualified to file and entitled to the benefits of the Bankruptcy Act. The petition is then notarized, establishing that you are who and what you say you are.

The next form is Schedule A—statements of all debts of bankruptcy. Here's where you list everybody you owe anything to: name, address, nature of claim and specific amount. The first on the list are the creditors having priorities:

A. Wages and commissions owed to workers, full- or part-time, not exceeding $600 to each, earned within three months before you file the bankruptcy petition.
B. Taxes owed to the United States, to any state or to any other taxing authority.
C. Debts owed to any person specifically having been authorized by United States law as having priority.
D. Rent owed to a landlord, accrued within three months of filing (in states that give this a priority).

Next is a list of creditors holding security, a description of the security and an estimate of market value or amount of security held.

Finally comes the big list: creditors having unsecured claims without priority. This is everybody you owe who hasn't been covered by one of the above categories. You'll need the name, the address, a description of the claim and the amount of money.

Following the information on what you owe and to whom is the disclosure of what you own that can be converted into cash to help repay the creditors. This begins with a list of real property and goes on into personal property. In the information given to persons filing bankruptcy in the Southern District of New York, the term "property" is defined as including "furniture, fixtures, machinery, equipment, automobiles, stocks, bonds, accounts receivable, money owed to you, income tax refunds, real estate and everything else you owned, possessed or had or which was coming to you on the date the bankruptcy was filed."

The final listing is of property you are claiming to be exempt, and thus not available to be used to repay the creditors. Each state has its own list of exempt properties, which is available to you from the Bankruptcy Clerk's office at the federal courthouse nearest you.

The New York State exemptions read as though they are from another century. One set of rules is for women and householders, and another set for men (nonhouseholders). At the top of the women-and-householders list is, "all stoves . . . and the necessary fuel for 60 days; one sewing machine with its appurtenances; the family Bible, family pictures and school books . . . not exceeding fifty dollars in value . . ."

The list goes on with "a seat or pew occupied by the judgement debtor of the family in a public place of worship," and "one radio receiver, a wedding ring and a watch not exceeding thirty-five dollars in value." Alimony and child support are exempt from bankruptcy action, and the householder is allowed to claim the exemption of a "homestead, a lot of land with one or more buildings thereon, not exceeding two thousand dollars in value."

At any rate, get the list of exemptions from your state and use them as a guide to filling in the forms.

The final form is a summary of the debts and the properties, totals taken from the other sheets. It is this summary that forms the working part of the bankruptcy—showing what is owed, and what is available to liquidate into money and pay off the creditors. The truth of the summary sheets is sworn before a notary. Then all forms, with the proper number of copies, are filed in the Bankruptcy Clerk's office. Some portion of the fee must be included, and/or the request for installment payments.

In Chapter Four, straight bankruptcy, the court calls a meeting between you and all the creditors you have listed. A time period is allotted for each creditor to file a claim against you, presenting the facts on what they think you owe them.

At the meeting a trustee is appointed by the judge or is elected by the creditors to be the manager of the proceedings. He or she is responsible for liquidating the estate, generally through an auction sale. An appraiser and auctioneer are sometimes appointed. Each of the creditors has a chance to speak, and the court and trustee will question you about your assets and debts.

After the first meeting the court issues orders to you, sent by mail, with copies to the trustee and to your lawyer, if you have one. The orders tell you how to proceed: to turn your money and property over to the trustee, or to supply additional information. When you get the orders, you must contact the trustee and fulfill your part of the arrangement.

The property is converted into cash by the trustee and distributed among the creditors who file proofs of claim. The expenses of the administration of your assets are also paid out of this cash. When the distribution is carried out, all fees are paid and any nonexempt debts are accounted for, the procedure is completed. It can take from several months to several years, depending on the size of the business and the complications.

If you are requesting a Chapter Eleven bankruptcy, it's a different story. You file the kit of forms listing all the creditors and your assets. The court calls a meeting, and the creditors elect a creditors' committee to manage the case. The creditors' committee works out an agreement among all the creditors saying they will accept proportionate settlements from you on the money you owe them. The settlement might be 10 cents on each dollar owed, or 50 cents on each dollar—the amount is suited to the facts you and they present.

The committee solicits all the creditors' acceptances, needing a majority of them to agree on the percentage of money. Payment schedules are worked out, and you continue operating your business, hoping to meet the payments and reorganize everything so you can begin to make a profit. In other words, Chapter Eleven is designed to help you get out of the red and into the black.

This chapter does not attempt to answer all questions about bankruptcy; it merely outlines the process in simplified form. Business bankruptcy is usually complicated. If the creditors having priorities—i.e., taxes and wages—cannot be satisfied, the debts you owe them continue as your personal liabilities, to be paid off out of future work you do.

Most business bankruptcies are best handled by an attorney, whether or not the business is incorporated. Fees in the New York area begin around $300 to $400 for a simple situation, and increase for larger and more complex cases. Legal Aid can rarely be of assistance to a business but sometimes is able to help on no-asset personal bankruptcies.

The most frequent reason bankruptcies are denied their discharge or have their discharge taken away is failure to obey orders sent them by the court. If you don't understand or don't agree with orders you receive, act *immediately* to have the circumstance clarified. Don't wait. Orders can be contested or explained more fully, but it's up to you to take the initiative.

Also, it is your responsibility to stay in touch with the

court, to cooperate with the trustee or the creditor's committee, and to make sure everybody can find you when they want to. Changes of address and phone must be filed by mail with the court.

Enough of going out of business; if it happens, it happens. Learn from it. And now listen to some retailers tell about their beginnings—there's a lot to learn from them, too.

The Toy Works, Minneapolis, Minnesota

According to Joan and Orrel Thompson, people are always looking in the windows of The Toy Works. Customers look for awhile and then say to each other, "Gee, I had one of those when I was a kid." Which is exactly the response the Thompsons hope for because the shop is designed with nostalgia in mind.

The Toy Works has been open for business for four years, and The American Sampler, a spin-off shop, made it's debut a year ago. Both are located in a fabulous renovated warehouse in downtown Minneapolis; a huge structure that has won many architecture and landmark awards and is favorably compared to San Francisco's Ghirardelli Square. Butler Square is filled with delightful small shops, restaurants, galleries, and is a pleasant place to visit in a pleasant city.

The decision to become shopkeepers came naturally to the Thompsons. Joan's background as an elementary educator was supplemented by working in a children's shop during college. Orrel's family ran country stores in southern Minnesota where he worked during summer vacations. His hobby has always been toymaking, with balance toys his specialty. Orrel's career includes managing museum gift shops, administrative positions at the Contemporary Art Museum in Akron, Ohio, and an associate directorship at the Art Institute in Minneapolis.

Prior to The Toy Works, Joan, Orrel and their four children would pile into their VW bus each weekend and travel around the country looking for folk art, antiques and other collectables. There was a running family joke about opening a shop or design center as their personal collection grew and grew. Finally in January, 1974, friends convinced the Thompsons to open their own store featuring Orrel's balance toys and many of their countryside finds.

The focus became clearer as the planning got underway. Yes, a toy store, but one that would carry only items that the Thompsons liked well enough to want to collect themselves. No war toys, and no TV or licensed toys. The test on merchandise was, "Do we really *love* it?" If the answer was a hearty "yes" then the item was in.

The restoration/renovation of Butler Square was just being completed, so the Thompsons visited it as part of their search for the right location. They decided immediately that The Toy Works belonged in Butler Square, and hastened to sign up for a choice first floor location. Since the building was new, their lease terms were extremely liberal: five years with an option to renew, and no percentage fee on their yearly income.

Their initial capitalization was a meager $5,000 of which $4,000 went into inventory. The other thousand covered pre-opening expenses. They arrived on Day One with no cash reserves. However, they had both decided to keep their jobs in order to support The Toy Works, regarding the shop as an extension of their hobby rather than a full-time endeavor. The Toy Works required some financial support for the first two years, with their lives becoming more and more shop-centered as the business developed.

Since their budget was so limited, Orrel built the interior himself, drawing on his art background to design a system of planks and crates that furnished superb flexibility and was in keeping with the look of their merchandise.

No pre-opening advertising or promotion budget was feasible. Recognizing the need for spreading the word, the Thompsons embarked on a campaign to do their own publicity. Their efforts were successful. They appeared as guests on local talk shows and got written up as "interesting local people doing interesting things" in various publications in the Minneapolis/St. Paul area.

Eventually they did try some advertising but found it wasn't as effective as direct mail for their particular customers. Every other year is their tentative schedule for major mailings; a slower pace than most direct mail programs, but one that takes into consideration that their merchandise is rather special and customers' tastes must be developed.

The American Sampler shop was opened to present the non-toy parts of the Thompson's personal collections—and because they could find no Minneapolis gallery that dealt with American folk art. Located in Butler Square, a floor below The Toy Works, American Sampler is set up to display merchandise and also to house exhibitions in a traditional gallery sense. Orrel sees American Sampler as a transitional venture and is already putting out feelers into other areas.

Concentrated direct mail selling is being explored for American Sampler. The first try was a mailing directed to interior decorators and architects in ten counties surrounding Minneapolis. The mailing list was purchased from the direct mail house that now handles all their business. The plan is to do a series of staggered mailings every two to four weeks, expanding as the audience increases.

In his forecast for the future, Orrel sees several branches of The Toy Works, perhaps in other parts of the country, and says they are keeping an open mind as to the future of American Sampler. "At the moment it looks like American Sampler will turn into a gallery, but you never can tell. Intuition has always been a big part of our decision making. We're just going to watch the store's progress and trust that we'll know when the right moment has arrived."

As to advice for novice retailers, the Thompsons suggest that priority be given to the hiring of an accountant to set up the entire financial system well before Day One. Orrel said that was a major mistake they made—trying to set up their own system, and it took them two years to untangle everything, with the help of a good accountant.

"And," Orrel adds with a grin, "keep in mind there are three very important factors for specialty shop owners—location, Location, and LOCATION."

Mushroom Crafts, Key Largo, Florida

Route One stretches south from Miami to Key West, connecting the many little islands that form the Florida Keys. It is not the only road in the Keys but it is by far the major road and the logical place for any business, large or small.

Mushroom Crafts, Inc., is located in a modern two-story building near the shopping mall at Key Largo. Signs depicting huge, fairytale mushrooms alert motorists to the shop. "We were looking for a name that was a little different and sounded pleasant," says owner Shirley Baad. "Somebody suggested mushroom craft and it seemed right for us. People collect mushroom pictures and figurines; in fact sometimes people stop in just because of the name."

The Baad family came to Florida from Ohio in 1962. Robert Baad's job with the telephone company located them in Key Largo, the first large settlement in the Keys south of Miami. Crafts had always been the main hobby for Shirley and their three small children. They soon found they had to drive all the way up to Miami to buy supplies, which led Shirley to speculate about the idea of opening a crafts shop.

As a busy young mother she didn't have time to do much else but think about opening a shop, but as the children grew older she became serious about it. Her mother-in-law, a skilled potter, joined them and reinforced Shirley's thinking. She had worked in crafts shops and was experienced in crafts teaching and retailing.

Their knowledge of the Keys helped in the final decision to go into business. A popular tourist area, Key Largo has a large winter population of retired people plus a sizeable group of tourist "widows" whose husbands come to the Keys for deep sea fishing. If promoted carefully, the shop would have a ready clientele for workshops, classes and supplies.

Shirley sent for some of the informative booklets available from the Small Business Administration. The opening a shop project became a family affair, and the excitement mounted. Husband Robert became Shirley's silent partner, and $11,000 was allocated from their savings to capitalize the venture.

What spurred them on was the construction of a building on the highway near the shopping center. The Baads checked it out, and rented the first floor store on a two-year lease with an option to renew. They have since renewed for five more years.

The lease-signing was two and a half months prior to their opening date, but since the building was still under construction no rent was charged. The space was leased to them "as is" which meant they had to finish the floors and do the interior.

In the year prior to opening Mushroom Crafts, Shirley had been compiling data on suppliers and resources. Every trip to Miami resulted in more names of companies—often copied right off the labels found in the crafts departments. A crafts shop had opened down in Key West so the Baads visited there, became friendly and began to exchange business information.

They found most of the craft supplies are purchased through distributors located in Miami, St. Petersburg and Fort Lauderdale. Most of the distributors were willing to establish a limited amount of credit immediately. A few requested C.O.D. terms on the initial orders.

Periodically the distributors hold workshops to introduce new products and up-date standard sellers. Shirley found the workshops very helpful, not only for product and technique information but as a way to learn the language of the crafts retailer.

In addition to establishing a solid pre-opening inventory of craft supplies, Shirley worked out her first series of classes. These were short-term workshops planned for winter tourists. They were an immediate success and have been a vital part of the shop ever since. Shirley patterned the classes after similar workshops offered in Miami and Key West. Most of the introductory classes have no instruction fee. The shop's profit lies in the sale of materials. There is a charge for advanced technique classes, the amount varying if the instruction is individual or group.

Advertising played a large part in the pre-opening activities and was continued throughout the first year. In addition to newspapers and magazines, Shirley took ads in local campground brochures, pamphlets sent out by the Key Largo bank, and other community newsletters. Every attempt was made to coordinate with Girl Scout and Boy Scout troops, school and church organizations.

Despite all the planning and promotion the first two years of Mushroom Crafts are described by Shirley as "very trying." The gas shortage became a national problem during their initial months and resulted in a serious reduction in tourist traffic throughout the Keys. The local economy, dependent on the tourists, tightened up immediately, further reducing the amount of local resident business.

By the second year, national economists were referring to the country as being in a "recession" which was felt sharply in tourist areas. Consequently, the Baad family not only worked in the shop, they also supported it until conditions loosened up. Shirley feels that they have been on solid footing every since and hopes to continue. The major change has been the advertising budget. Now Mushroom Crafts does minimal advertising, depending on word-of-mouth publicity and connections with organizations to bring in business.

Shirley Baad's advice to people thinking about opening a shop focuses on commitment and determination. "You really have to want to do it. It takes lots of effort, more than anything else I can think of. You have to be determined. There's no way to foresee events so you just have to hang in there. And it can't be halfway. Either you jump in with both feet—or you stay out."

She feels that it would have been a bit easier for her if she had worked in somebody else's shop before opening her own. "I could have learned from others first so I'd have known more what to expect."

Her talk returns to money as the decisive factor for new retailers. "I didn't have a truly disastrous money situation because my husband had a good outside income. Without that, things would have been a lot different."

As to the future of Mushroom Crafts, Shirley wants it all to continue pretty much as it is. She expects to expand the needlepoint and stitchery department within the coming year in response to increased customer inquiries. "We are constantly adding new crafts and materials as they come on the market. That's fun and about as much expansion as I want. I'm content with things as they are."

Johnny Jupiter, New York City, New York

"My family had nothing to do with retailing, but I think my fascination with shops goes way back to when I was four years old. My family lived on a busy city block. By that age I was allowed to go out alone, and one day I discovered a funny old antique shop down the street from our building. The windows were covered with cobwebs, and inside was a jumble of magnificent things.

"Each day I would go to the shop and spend hours looking in the dusty window. It was a fantasy place and I felt I was looking into one of those wonderful Easter eggs that has a scene inside it. I had no idea one could go into the shop since it was always closed when I was there. But I would stand, day after day, enchanted with the dim, exotic world on the other side of the window.

"When I was five we moved and I never saw the antique shop again, but I was smitten. From then on I played store, I was the kid who always had the lemonade stand and, in my teens, decided on retail merchandising as a career."

This career choice took Jerry Harmyk into his mid-30's as a merchandiser for a nationally known furniture company. His college courses included three dimensional design studies which proved invaluable in presenting related items to customers.

After eight years with the furniture company Jerry found himself angry and disillusioned. He had little faith in the integrity of the organization; the products were sub-standard and selling was viewed as putting something over on the customer. Also he knew the company's profits were exhorbitantly high while his salary was mediocre. It was clearly time for him to move on.

Jerry took stock of his assets. He knew the furniture and accessories market and had spent his spare time browsing in local flea markets and antique shops. He had also renovated a small house in Pennsylvania in which he lived, doing much of the building himself. And he knew he never wanted to sell a product in which he had no faith.

He sold his house, took the money and headed for New York City. He found a small empty store on a corner in Greenwich Village that instinct told him was the right place for him. He signed a two-year lease on September 1, 1977 and worked around the clock creating a fantasy environment to house home furnishings, cooking equipment, antiques, toys, printed material and anything else that captured his fancy. A month and a half later, on October 15th, he opened for business, calling the shop Johnny Jupiter.

Jerry's pre-opening budget was $10,000, a sizeable portion of which he put into the interior. He built old fashioned wooden counters, shelves and even a small Victorian cupola over the front door. The rest of the money went into inventory, filling up the small shop to overflowing.

Crowded closeness was his intention; the floor plan centered around one aisle 2½' wide and 20' long. The shop comfortably holds four to six customers at a time. The small space, large inventory and stylized, handbuilt interior all adds up to an intriguing fantasy environment. Shopping at Johnny Jupiter is like a visit to some other time and place. During the holidays lines of customers stretch around the corner, patiently waiting their turn to get in the magic door.

By the morning of opening day Jerry had spent every cent of his money. To his dismay he found he didn't have enough cash left to buy himself breakfast so he opened the shop and hoped somebody would come along quick and buy something. Somebody did, so he locked up, ran across to the deli and returned to open up more officially. Lunch was handled in a similar manner but by dinner time people were crowding into Johnny Jupiter and Jerry knew he was going to be all right.

Jerry's merchandising approach centers on his displays. He did no pre-opening advertising, does no mailings or other promotion and has no telephone in the shop. He uses his two large windows as his advertising, changing the entire window display theme every week and refurbishing the entire store for every holiday. He moves quickly. The morning after Christmas Jerry is in the store sweeping out Christmas and ushering in a silver and champagne New Year.

There is no display budget as such since everything on display is for sale. All efforts center around creating a constantly changing magical world, perfect down to the most minute detail. Jerry is convinced that the most unassuming item can be improved by placing it in interesting surroundings. He always unpacks pre-packed items, common among kitchen utensils, so every piece can be out and touchable. The most mundane measuring spoon takes on new authority at Johnny Jupiter.

The weekly window displays have become a local legend, bringing Jerry the word-of-mouth publicity he feels is most effective. He received the 1977 Grand Award of Merit from the Greenwich Village Chamber of Commerce for Johnny Jupiter's Christmas windows. The display was the Little Match Girl, standing in the snow, looking into a second shop window that was filled with Christmas goodies.

Jerry Harmyk has a reality five-year plan and a fantasy five-year plan for the shop. In reality, he will probably open an uptown branch store, as small in scale as the Greenwich Village shop, utilizing the same approach. In fantasy, Jerry would have the world's smallest department store, housed in a slender New York brownstone. An ornate birdcage elevator would ferry customers up the outside of the house to floors devoted to kitchen equipment, toys, charcuterie and more.

He is more down to earth in advice to beginning retailers. Jerry feels small shop owners must guard against trying to be too chic and stocking all sorts of improbable items. The public is too smart to be taken in by such a put-on. Substitute exciting displays for far-out merchandise and real, functional stock takes on new allure.

"The store policy at Johnny Jupiter sounds a bit corny," says Jerry, "but the customer is always right. Refunds and exchanges are done quickly and cheerfully. It's something I feel strongly about and it has paid off. I've never been happier in my life. My store is something I'm really fond of."

Canal Towne Emporium, Wurtsboro, New York

"I've always loved this building," said Doris Holmes, glancing around the main room of her shop. "My husband's grandfather ran a country store here in the 1840s. At that time the D. & H. Canal went from Honesdale, Pennsylvania to Kingston, New York, and the country store was a stop along the route. When the canal ceased operating, the store continued and my husband remembers working in it after school and on weekends. Eventually the store closed but the building remained in the family. We inherited it—and I was rarin' to go!"

Opening a shop represented a second career change for Doris. She had gone back to school when her two sons were eleven and thirteen, gotten a degree in social work and was a full-time social worker who collected antiques as a hobby. "Everybody thought I was nuts when I decided to open the Emporium. My life was just getting settled," she claims.

Her family took a bit of convincing. Once won over, her husband, a local banker, helped form the corporation and the two of them began a two year stint renovating the old building. During that time Doris continued working and both the Holmes' researched shops and collected resources, often from the labels on merchandise they admired.

The initial capital was raised in an interesting way. Since they owned the building and some adjacent land in downtown Wurtsboro, the Holmes' were able to take out a mortgage for $40,000. This gave them money to execute the renovation and to put $27,000 into pre-opening inventory; $5,000 was set aside in the bank as operating capital.

Doris says she feels now that the amount of money was exactly right for what she visualized. "We could have done it on less money, but not as successfully. I knew just what I wanted. I could even see the interior of the store in my mind's eye. Less initial capital would have meant smaller inventory, a much more marginal operation and constant money worries."

The do-it-yourself renovations had a side benefit: everybody in the small town of Wurtsboro was in on the Emporium from the beginning. Sidewalk superintending became a local hobby and the community seemed to be rooting for Doris as the opening date approached.

May 29th, 1976, was selected for Day One. An ad was placed in the local newspaper and Doris and her kids made up brochures which they put around in nearby resort hotels. Friends and wellwishers were invited to a big party held in the shop the night before the official opening.

On the morning of the 29th, the Wurtsboro Drum and

Bugle Corps surprised Doris by marchng up to the Emporium door and serenading her with their version of "It's A Small World." By the time the music ended there were about a hundred people waiting to get in, and the Emporium was officially in business.

The shop was a success from the start, but Doris kept her social work job for the first six months just in case. A part-time clerk was hired, and her oldest son was paid a small salary. The rest of the time the family just pitched in.

Wurtsboro is in the heart of the Catskill Mountain resort area, near to Route 17, a major road, so the Holmes' advertising and promotion plans focused not only on local customers but also on attracting vacationers and tourists. Small ads are run regularly in the Hudson Valley Magazine and in the Saturday edition of the local newspaper. The largest part of their promotion budget is spent on a large billboard sign out on Route 17.

"It costs me $1,800 a year, which nearly floored me at first, but it's worth it," explained Doris. "Actually this is our second billboard. The first sign we took was nine miles away from the Wurtsboro exit. It was the only one available at that time but it proved to be too far away from the turn-off. Our current sign is four miles away and it's perfect." The billboard is done in quaint old lettering (but very readable) and includes the fact that the Emporium is easily reached, just a few minutes off and back onto the highway.

When discussing her stock Doris says she tried to take items on consignment when the shop was new but has phased it out except for a small amount of unusual craft items. She prefers to purchase her inventory outright, guided by her instinct and knowledge of her customers' tastes. The inventory is extremely varied, as befits a country store, Handcrafted furniture and accessories fill the second floor of the shop, while downstairs is divided into areas featuring bolts of calico, penny candy, coffees and teas, kitchenware, clothing, stationery, quilts and other delights.

Canal Towne Emporium is noted for it's active program of community events and its stylized country store newsletter passed out to all visitors. Doris says it all started with a friend of hers who does marvelous flower arrangements using seasonal, local materials. They decided to try an afternoon demonstration/lecture which was so successful it was repeated several times. A quilt show and sale was next, featuring the work of a talented local designer. Now such "specials" are a part of each month's activities.

An area that Doris Holmes is exploring now is direct mail selling. Last May she put her first ad in *Yankee* magazine, a publication with a good track record for direct mail items. The ad pulled well, so her plan is to continue slowly and enclose flyers of similar items in the packages she sends out. By combining the ads and the flyers Doris expects to eventually build up a mailing list and perhaps, in the distant future, come out with a catalogue.

Her forecast for the next five years is that the shop will grow in size, perhaps building out onto some of the adjacent land. A larger staff is in the planning, perhaps to service the growing direct mail business.

Doris doesn't want any branch stores; her feeling for the old building still holds sway. She mentions the possibility of a restaurant or tea shop as part of the expansion, saying that many customers have suggested it and she is interested.

Doris's advice to would-be retailers: "Be careful of your budgets. It's so easy to overspend. My husband is excellent as a business partner. He keeps me on a budget—and I know I'd have trouble doing that myself."

SUGGESTED READING

Stand Up, Speak Out, Talk Back! by Robert E. Alberti and Michael L. Emmons, Pocket Books (paperback), New York, 1975.

How To Be An Assertive (Not Aggressive) Woman by Jean Baer, Rawson Associates, New York, 1976.

The New Assertive Woman by Lynn Z. Bloom and Karen Coburn, Dell Books (paperback), New York, 1976.

Don't Say Yes When You Want To Say No by Jean Baer and Herbert Fensterheim, Dell Books (paperback), New York, 1975.

When I Say No I Feel Guilty by Manuel J. Smith, Bantam Books (paperback), New York, 1975.

Looking Out For Number One by Robert J. Ringer, Funk & Wagnalls, New York, 1976.

The Art of Selfishness by David Seabury, Pocket Books (paperback), New York, 1968.

SBA Field Offices

Addresses and Telephone Numbers

City	State	Zip Code	Address	Telephone
Boston	Mass.	02114	150 Causeway St., 10th Floor	(617) 223-2100
Boston	Mass.	02114	150 Causeway St., 10th Floor	(617) 223-2100
Holyoke	Mass	01040	302 High St., 4th Floor	(413) 536-8770
Augusta	Maine	04330	Federal Bldg., 40 Western Ave., Room 512	(207) 622-6171
Concord	N.H.	03301	55 Pleasant St., Room 213	(603) 224-4041
Hartford	Conn.	06103	One Financial Plaza	(203) 244-3600
Montpelier	Vt.	05602	Federal Bldg., 87 State St., Room 210	(802) 223-7472
Providence	R.I.	02903	57 Eddy St., 7th Floor	(401) 528-1000
New York	N.Y.	10007	26 Federal Plaza, Room 3214	(212) 264-1468
New York	N.Y.	10007	26 Federal Plaza, Room 3100	(212) 264-4355
Melville	N.Y.	11746	425 Broad Hollow Rd. Room 205	(516) 752-1626
Hato Rey	Puerto Rico	00919	Cardon and Bolivia Streets, PO Box 1915	(809) 763-6363
St. Thomas	Virgin Island	00801	Franklin Bldg.	(809) 774-1331
Newark	N.J.	07102	970 Broad St., Room 1635	(201) 645-2434
Camden	N.J.	08104	1800 East Davis St.	(609) 757-5183
Syracuse	N.Y.	13202	Federal Bldg., 100 South Clinton St., Room 1073	(315) 473-3314
Buffalo	N.Y.	14202	Federal Bldg., 111 West Huron St.,	(716) 842-3240
Elmira	N.Y.	14901	180 State St., Room 412	(607) 733-4686
Albany	N.Y.	12210	Twin Towers Bldg., 99 Washington Ave., Room 921	(518) 472-6300
Rochester	N.Y.	14614	Federal Bldg., 100 State St.	(716) 263-6700
Philadelphia	Bala Cynwyd, Pa.	19004	231 Asaphs Rd., 1 Bala Cynwyd Plaza, Suite 646 West Lobby	(215) 597-3311
Philadelphia	Bala Cynwyd, Pa.	19004	231 St. Asaphs Rd., 1 Bala Cynwyd Plaza, Suite 400 East Lobby	(215) 597-3311
Harrisburg	Pa.	17102	1500 North 2nd St.	(717) 782-3840
Wilkes-Barre	Pa.	18702	Penn Place, 20 N. Pennsylvania Ave.	(717) 826-6497
Wilmington	Del.	19801	Federal Bldg., 844 King St., Room 5207, Lockbox 16	(302) 571-6294
Baltimore	Towson Md.	21204	7800 York Rd.	(301) 962-2150
Clarksburg	W. Va.	26301	Lowndes Bldg., 109 North 3rd St., Room 301	(304) 623-5631
Charleston	W. Va.	25301	Charleston National Plaza, Suite 628	(304) 343-6181
Pittsburgh	Pa.	15222	Federal Bldg., 1000 Liberty Ave., Room 1401	(412) 644-2780
Richmond	Va.	23240	Federal Bldg., 400 North 8th St., Room 3015	(804) 782-2617
Washington	D.C.	20417	1030 15th St. N.W., Suite 250	(202) 655-4000

City	State	ZIP	Address	Phone
Atlanta	Ga.	30309	1401 Peachtree St., N.E., Room 470	(404) 881-4943
Atlanta	Ga.	30309	1720 Peachtree St., N.E., 6th Floor	(404) 881-4325
Birmingham	Ala.	35205	908 South 20th St., Room 202	(205) 254-1344
Charlotte	N.C.	28202	230 S. Tryon St.	(704) 372-0711
Greenville	N.C.	27834	215 South Evans St., Room 206	(919) 752-3798
Columbia	S.C.	29201	1801 Assembly St., Room 131	(803) 765-5376
Jackson	Miss.	39201	Petroleum Bldg., 200 E. Pascagoula St., Suite 690	(601) 969-4371
Biloxi	Miss.	39530	111 Fred Haise Blvd., 2nd Floor, Gulf Nat. Life Insurance Bldg.	(601) 435-3676
Jacksonville	Fla.	32202	Federal Bldg., 400 West Bay St., Room 261, PO Box 35067	(904) 791-3782
Louisville	Ky.	40201	Federal Bldg., 600 Federal Pl., Room 188	(502) 582-5971
Miami	Coral Gables Fla.	33134	2222 Ponce De Leon Blvd., 5th Floor	(305) 350-5521
Tampa	Fla.	33607	1802 N. Trask St., Suite 203	(813) 228-2594
Nashville	Tenn.	37219	404 James Robertson Pkwy., Suite 1012	(615) 749-5881
Knoxville	Tenn.	37902	Fidelity Bankers Bldg., 502 South Gay St., Room 307	(615) 637-9300
Memphis	Tenn.	38103	Federal Bldg., 167 North Main St., Room 211	(901) 521-3588
West Palm Beach	Fla.	33402	Federal Bldg., 701 Clematis St., Room 229	(305) 659-7533
Chicago	Ill.	60604	Federal Bldg., 219 South Dearborn St., Room 838	(312) 353-0355
Chicago	Ill.	60604	Federal Bldg., 219 South Dearborn St., Room 437	(312) 353-4528
Springfield	Ill.	62701	One North, Old State Capital Plaza	(217) 525-4416
Cleveland	Ohio	44199	1240 East 9th St., Room 317	(216) 522-4180
Columbus	Ohio	43215	Tonti Bldg., 34 North High Street	(614) 469-6860
Cincinnati	Ohio	45202	Federal Bldg., 440 Main St.	(513) 684-2814
Detroit	Mich.	48226	McNamara Bldg., 477 Michigan Ave.	(313) 226-6075
Marquette	Mich.	49855	Don H. Bottum University Center, 540 W. Kaye Ave.	(906) 255-1108
Indianapolis	Ind.	46204	New Federal Bldg., 575 North Pennsylvania St., Room 552	(317) 269-7272
Madison	Wis.	53703	122 West Washington Ave., Room 713	(608) 252-5261
Milwaukee	Wis.	53233	Continental Bank Bldg., 735 West Wisconsin Ave., Room 690	(414) 224-3941
Eau Claire	Wis.	54701	Federal Office Bldg. & U.S. Courthouse, 500 South Barstow St., Room B9AA	(715) 834-9012
Minneapolis	Minn.	55402	Plymouth Bldg., 12 South 6th St.	(612) 725-2362
Dallas	Tex.	75235	Regal Park Office Bldg., 1720 Regal Row, Suite 230	(214) 749-2531
Dallas	Tex.	75202	1100 Commerce St., Room 300	(214) 749-1011
Marshall	Tex.	75670	Federal Bldg. G-12, 100 South Washington St.	(214) 935-5257
Albuquerque	N.Mex.	87110	Patio Plaza Bldg., 5000 Marble Ave., N.E.	(505) 766-3430
Houston	Tex.	77002	One Allen Ctr., 500 Dallas	(713) 226-4341
Little Rock	Ark.	72201	611 Gaines St., Suite 900	(501) 378-5871
Lubbock	Tex.	79408	712 Federal Office Bldg. & U.S. Courthouse, 1205 Texas Ave.	(806) 762-7011
El Paso	Tex.	79901	4100 Bravo, Suite 300	(915) 543-7200
Lower Rio Grande Valley	Harlingen, Tex.	78550	222 East Van Buren St.	(512) 423-3011
Corpus Christi	Tex.	78408	3105 Leopard St.	(512) 888-3011

City	State	Address	ZIP	Phone
New Orleans	La.	Plaza Tower, 1001 Howard Ave., 17th Floor	70113	(504) 589-2611
Shreveport	La.	U.S. Post Office & Courthouse Building, Fannin St.	71163	(318) 226-5196
Oklahoma City	Okla.	50 Penn Pl., Suite 840	73118	(405) 736-4011
San Antonio	Tex.	727 E. Durango, Room A-513	78206	(512) 229-6250
Kansas City	Mo.	911 Walnut St., 23rd Floor	64106	(186) 374-3318
Kansas City	Mo.	1150 Grande Ave., 5th Floor	64106	(816) 374-5557
Des Moines	Iowa	New Federal Bldg., 210 Walnut St., Room 749	50309	(515) 284-4422
Omaha	Neb.	Empire State Bldg., Nineteen and Farnam Sts.	68102	(402) 221-4691
St. Louis	Mo.	Mercantile Tower, One Mercantile Center Suite 2500	63101	(314) 425-4191
Wichita	Kan.	Main Place Bldg., 110 East Waterman St.	67202	(316) 267-6566
Denver	Colo.	Executive Tower Bldg., 1405 Curtis St.	80202	(303) 837-0111
Denver	Colo.	721 19th St., Room 426A	80202	(303) 837-0111
Casper	Wyo.	Federal Bldg., 100 East B St., Room 4001	82601	(307) 265-5550
Fargo	N.Dak.	Federal Bldg., 653 2nd Ave., North, Room 218	58102	(701) 783-5771
Helena	Mont.	618 Helena Ave.	59601	(406) 588-6011
Salt Lake City	Utah	Federal Bldg., 125 South St. St., Room 2237	84111	(801) 588-5500
Sioux Falls	S. Dak.	National Bank Bldg., 8th and Main Ave., Room 402	57102	(605) 336-2980
Rapid City	S. Dak.	Federal Bldg., 515 9th St., Room 246	57701	(605) 343-5074
San Francisco	Calif.	Federal Bldg., 450 Golden Gate Ave., Box 36044	94102	(415) 556-4530
San Francisco	Calif.	211 Main St.	94105	(415) 556-9000
Fresno	Calif.	Federal Bldg., 1130 O. St., Room 4015	93721	(209) 487-5000
Sacramento	Calif.	2800 Cottage Way	95825	(916) 484-4200
Las Vegas	Nev.	301 E. Stewart	89121	(702) 385-6011
Reno	Nev.	300 Booth St.	89504	(702) 784-5234
Honolulu	Hawaii	1149 Bethel St., Room 402	96813	*(808) 546-8950
Agana	Guam	Ada Plaza Center Bldg.	96910	* 777-8420
Los Angeles	Calif.	350 S. Figueroa St., 6th Floor	90071	(213) 688-2000
Phoenix	Ariz.	112 North Central Ave.	85004	(602) 261-3900
San Diego	Calif.	Federal Bldg., 880 Front St., Room 4-S-33	92188	(714) 293-5444
Seattle	Wash.	Dexter Horton Bldg., 710 2nd Ave., 5th Floor	98104	(206) 442-1455
Seattle	Wash.	Federal Bldg., 915 Second Ave., Room 1744	98174	(206) 442-5534
Anchorage	Alaska	Anchorage Legal Center, 1016 West 6th Ave., Suite 200	99501	*(907) 272-5561
Fairbanks	Alaska	501½ Second Ave.	99701	*(907) 452-1951
Boise	Idaho	216 North 8th St., Room 408	83701	(208) 554-1096
Portland	Oreg.	Federal Bldg., 1220 S.W. Third Ave.	97205	(503) 221-2682
Spokane	Wash.	Court House Bldg., Room 651	99210	(509) 456-2100

*Dial operator for assistance.

Advertising Information

The Advertising Council
825 Third Ave., New York, N.Y. 10022
Advertising Research Foundation
3 East 54th St., New York, N.Y. 10022
American Advertising Federation
1225 Connecticut Ave., N.W.
Washington, D.C. 20036
American Association of Advertising Agencies
200 Park Ave., New York, N.Y. 10017
American Marketing Association
222 Riverside Plaza, Chicago, Ill. 60606
Council of Better Business Bureaus
845 Third Ave., New York, N.Y. 10022
Direct Mail Marketing Association
6 East 43rd St., New York, N.Y. 10017
National Association of Broadcasters
1771 North Street N.W.
Washington, D.C. 20036
National Retail Merchants Association
100 West 31st St., New York, N.Y. 10022
Newspaper Advertising Bureau
485 Lexington Ave., New York, N.Y. 10017
Point-of-Purchase Advertising Institute
521 Fifth Ave., New York, N.Y. 10017
Television Bureau of Advertising
1 Rockefeller Plaza, New York, N.Y. 10022
Transit Advertising Association
1725 K Street, N.W., Washington, D.C. 20006

For a comprehensive list of trade publications, consult one of the following guides that are available for reference in most libraries:

Advertising Age
740 North Rush St., Chicago, Ill. 60611

N. W. Ayer and Son's Directory of Newspapers and Periodicals

Business Publications Rates and Data

Industrial Marketing Media-Marketing Planning Guide

National Trade and Professional Association of the U.S. and Canada Labor Unions

For further data on lighting:

Illuminating Engineering Society of North America
345 East 47th St.
New York, N.Y. 10017
(212) 644-7917

General Exemption Certificate

I hereby certify that this purchase is for resale in the regular course of business, or is to be used as an ingredient or component part of a new article of tangible personal property to be produced for sale.

Registration no. _____

Name as registered _____

Firm name _____

Address _____

Type of business _____

Authorized signature _____

Title _____

Date _____

OFFICE OF MINORITY BUSINESS ENTERPRISE
REGIONAL ORGANIZATIONS

Minorities eligible for direct assistance from programs administered by OMBE include, but not exclusively, Blacks, Puerto Ricans, Spanish-Speaking Americans, American Indians, Eskimos and Aleuts.

The United States is divided up into six regions. For further information, contact the office in your region:

Atlanta Region:

Charles McMillan, Regional Director, OMBE
U.S. Department of Commerce
1371 Peachtree St. N.E., Suite 505
Atlanta, Georgia, 30309. Phone: 404-881-5091

Atlanta Region includes the following States:
 Kentucky, Tennessee, North and South Carolina
 Georgia, Alabama, Mississippi and Florida.

Chicago Region:

Harold Jones, Acting Regional Director, OMBE
U.S. Department of Commerce
55 East Monroe Street, Suite 1438
Chicago, Ill., 60603. Phone: 312-353-8375

Chicago Region includes the following States:
 Minnesota, Wisconsin, Michigan, Ohio, Indiana,
 Illinois, Missouri, Kansas, Iowa and Nebraska

Dallas Region:

Henry Zuniga, Regional Director, OMBE
U.S. Department of Commerce

1412 Main Street, Room 1702
Dallas, Texas, 75202. Phone: 214-749-7581

Dallas Region includes:
Montana, North and South Dakota, Wyoming,
Utah, Colorado, New Mexico, Texas, Arkansas,
Oklahoma and Louisiana.

New York Region:

Newton S. Downing, Regional Director, OMBE
U.S. Department of Commerce
26 Federal Plaza, Room 1307
New York, N.Y. 10007. Phone: 212-264-3262

New York Region includes:
Maine, Vermont, New Hampshire, Massachusetts,
Connecticut, Rhode Island, New York, New Jersey,
Puerto Rico and the Virgin Islands

San Francisco Region:

Ramon V. Romero, Regional Director, OMBE
U.S. Department of Commerce
Federal Bldg., 450 Golden Gate Ave., Room 15045
San Francisco, California 94102. Phone: 415-556-7234

San Francisco Region includes:
Washington, Oregon, Idaho, Nevada, California,
Arizona, Alaska, Hawaii and American Samoa

Washington Region:

Luis Encinias, Regional Director, OMBE
U.S. Department of Commerce
1730 K Street, N.W. Suite 420
Washington, D.C. 20006. Phone: 202-634-7897

Washington Region includes:
Pennsylvania, Delaware, Maryland,
Virginia and West Virginia

Gallery
Agreement

AGREEMENT, made on this ___day of_____, 197__, between _____(hereinafter referred to as "the Gallery") and _____(hereinafter referred to as "the Artist").

1. The Gallery will present a show of works created by the Artist, at such time and for such length of time as the Gallery shall determine. The Gallery shall have the right to determine whether this show shall be an individual show or whether the Artist's works shall be included in a group show.

2. The Artist shall bear the cost of shipping the works to the Gallery and the cost of framing. The Gallery shall bear all other costs incident upon the show.

3. The Gallery may take works from the Artist on consignment or it may purchase such works from the Artist. When a work taken on consignment is sold, the Gallery shall be entitled to retain forty per cent (40%) of the sale price as its commission. In the case of purchase of a work by the Gallery, the Gallery and the Artist shall agree upon the price which the Gallery is to pay for the work and the price at which the work is to be sold by the Gallery.

4. In the event that the Gallery sells a work which is purchased from the Artist for more than the agreed upon sale price, the excess of the actual sale price over the agreed upon sale price shall be distributed as follows: forty per cent (40%) shall be retained by the Gallery, forty per cent (40%) shall be paid to the Artist, and twenty per

cent (20%) shall be paid into a fund for the development of the arts, to be administered by the Gallery.

5. The Gallery shall have the option to present a second show of the Artist's works at such time and for such length of time as the Gallery shall determine. Within sixty (60) days after the conclusion of the show provided for in paragraph 1 of this Agreement, the Gallery shall notify the Artist whether or not it will exercise its option to present a second show. If the Gallery does exercise this option, the Artist shall remain under contract to the Gallery until the conclusion of the second show of his/her works.

6. The second show, if it is presented, shall be governed by the same terms and conditions as the first show, as set forth in paragraphs 1 through 4 of this Agreement.

7. So long as this Agreement remains in force, the Gallery shall be the exclusive dealer of the Artist's works and the Artist may not sell such works through any other gallery, dealer or agent, except by the written consent of the Gallery. The Gallery shall have the right of first selection of works produced by the Artist, for inclusion in the show(s) which it will present. Any works not selected by the Gallery may be sold by the Artist; however, such sales shall be billed through the Gallery and the Gallery shall be entitled to retain twenty-five per cent (25%) of the sale price as its commission.

8. This Agreement shall remain in force from the date of its execution until sixty (60) days after the conclusion of the first show of the Artist's works or, if the Gallery exercises the option created by paragraph 5 of this Agreement, until sixty (60) days after the conclusion of the second

show of the Artist's works. In addition, the Gallery shall remain bound by the terms of paragraph 4 of this Agreement so long as it retains any works which it purchased from the Artist.

Dated: New York, New York
_____, 197

The   Gallery, Inc.
By _____

_____

VOLUNTEER LAWYERS FOR THE ARTS
ORGANIZATIONS

New York City:

James J. Fishman
Volunteer Lawyers for the Arts
36 West 44th Street
New York, New York 10036
(212) 575-1150

New York State Branch Offices:

Albany:

Carol Bullard
Albany League of the Arts, Inc.
135 Washington Avenue
Albany, New York 12210
(518) 449-5380

Buffalo:

Maxine Brandenburg
Arts Development Services
237 Main Street
Buffalo, New York 14203
(716) 856-7520

Glens Falls:

Robert J. Kafin
115 Maple Street
Glens Fall, New York 12801
(518) 793-6631

Huntington:

Cindy Kiebitz
Huntington Area Arts Council, Inc.
12 New Street
Huntington, New York 11743
(516) 271-8423

Oneonta:

Leonard Ryndes
Upper Catskill Community Council of the Arts, Inc.
101 Old Milne Library
State University College
Oneonta, New York 13820
(607) 432-2070

Poughkeepsie:

Naj Wycoff
Dutchess County Arts Council
Cunneen-Hackett Cultural Center
9 Vassar Street
Poughkeepsie, New York 12601
(914) 454-3222

Rochester:

McCrea Hazlett
Arts Council of Rochester, Inc.
930 East Avenue
Rochester, New York 14607
(716) 442-0570

Nationwide:

Boston:

Linda McKinney
Lawyers for the Arts
Massachusetts Council on the Arts and Humanities
100 Boylston Street
Boston, Massachusetts 02116
(617) 732-3851

Chicago:

Lawyers for the Creative Arts
111 North Wabash
Chicago, Illinois 60602
(312) 263-6989

Cleveland:

Volunteer Lawyers for the Arts
c/o Cleveland Area Arts Council
108 The Arcade
Cleveland, Ohio 44114
(216) 781-0045

Connecticut:

Rand Foreman
Connecticut Commission on the Arts
340 Capitol Avenue
Hartford, Connecticut 06106
(203) 566-4770

Dallas:

Jay M. Vogelson
Steinberg, Generes, Luerssen & Vogelson
2200 Fidelity Union Tower
Dallas, Texas 75201
(214) 748-9312

Georgia:

Robert C. Lower
Georgia Volunteer Lawyers for the Arts, Inc.
c/o Alston, Miller & Gaines
1200 C & S National Bank Building
Atlanta, Georgia 30303
(404) 588-0300

Los Angeles:

Audrey Greenberg
Advocates for the Arts
Law School, Room 2467C
University of California
Los Angeles, California 90024
(213) 825-3309 or (213) 825-4841

New Jersey:

Harry Devlin
Cultural Law Committee
New Jersey State Bar Association
Trenton, New Jersey 08608
(201) 232-2323

Oregon:

Leonard Du Boff
Lewis and Clark College
Northwestern School of Law
Portland, Oregon 97219
(503) 244-1181

Philadelphia:

Ned Donohue
3400 Centre Square West
1500 Market Street
Philadelphia, Pennsylvania 19102
(215) 972-3539

Providence:

Stephen T. O'Neill
Rhode Island Volunteer Lawyers for the Arts
c/o Adler Pollock & Sheehan
One Hospital Trust Plaza
Providence, Rhode Island 02903
(401) 274-7200

San Francisco:

Hamish Sandison
Bay Area Lawyers for the Arts
25 Taylor Street
San Francisco, California 94102
(415) 775-7200

Washington, D.C.–Maryland:

Joshua Kaufman
Lawyers Committee for the Arts
8728 Colesville Road, Suite 1201
Silver Springs, Maryland 20910
(301) 587-1002

Washington:

Barbara Hoffman
Washington Volunteer Lawyers for the Arts
University of Puget Sound Law School
55 Tacoma Way
Tacoma, Washington 98402
(206) 756-3327

London, England:

Artlaw Services, Ltd.
125 Shaftesbury Avenue
London WC2 England
01-240-0610

Index

Tourist-oriented shops, 28
Toy Works, The, 190-193
Trade, defined, 15
Trade magazines, 93, 179-180
Trade publications, 15-16, 208-209
Trade shows, 93-94
Traffic builders, 141-143
Trunk shows, 161
Tungsten-hologen lamps, 117

Unemployment taxes, 85, 88-89
U.S. Department of Agriculture, 58, 60
U.S.D.A. Economic Statistics & Cooperative Service, 58
U.S. Department of Commerce, 50
U.S. Department of Labor, 64

Vanity-type art galleries, 169-170
Vertical display space, 113-114
Volunteer Lawyers for the Arts, 177, 216-221

Walls, display considerations for, 114-115
Ware, Henry A., 100-101
W-4 forms, 87
Wholesale merchandise, 94-99
　　brokers, 98-99
　　buying offices, 97-98, 99
　　locating resources for, 93-94
　　method of payment, 95-97
　　placing orders, 94-95
　　quantity discounts, 94
Wholesale prices, 29
Women's apparel shop, merchandise category break-down for, 26-27
Women's Wear Daily, 15, 26
Workmen's compensation, 53, 64-65
W-2 form, 87

Zoning laws, 64